MW00387114

BEST LOVED
Family
Recipes

Favorite dishes that get your
family's seal of approval

pil

Publications International, Ltd.

Louis Weber, CEO
Publications International, Ltd.
8140 Lehigh Ave
Morton Grove, IL 60053

Permission is never granted for commercial purposes.

Photograph on front cover and page 125 © Shutterstock.com.

Art on interior pages © Shutterstock.com.

Pictured on the front cover: Macaroni and Cheese *(page 124)*.

Pictured on the back cover *(clockwise from top):* Ham and Swiss Biscuits *(page 22)*, French Dip Sandwiches *(page 104)*, Crispy Ranch Chicken *(page 67)* and Chocolate Eclair Cake *(page 176)*.

ISBN: 978-1-63938-455-6

Manufactured in China.

8 7 6 5 4 3 2 1

Microwave Cooking: Microwave ovens vary in wattage. Use the cooking times as guidelines and check for doneness before adding more time.

WARNING: Food preparation, baking and cooking involve inherent dangers: misuse of electric products, sharp electric tools, boiling water, hot stoves, allergic reactions, foodborne illnesses and the like, pose numerous potential risks. Publications International, Ltd. (PIL) assumes no responsibility or liability for any damages you may experience as a result of following recipes, instructions, tips or advice in this publication.

While we hope this publication helps you find new ways to eat delicious foods, you may not always achieve the results desired due to variations in ingredients, cooking temperatures, typos, errors, omissions or individual cooking abilities.

Let's get social!

 @Publications_International

 @PublicationsInternational

www.pilbooks.com

CONTENTS

BREAKFAST & BRUNCH

Strawberry Banana French Toast

MAKES 4 SERVINGS

2 cups sliced fresh strawberries

4 teaspoons granulated sugar

4 eggs

1 cup milk

1/3 cup all-purpose flour

1 teaspoon vanilla

1/4 teaspoon salt

2 tablespoons butter

8 slices (1 inch thick) egg bread or country bread

2 bananas, cut into 1/4-inch slices

Whipped cream and powdered sugar (optional)

Maple syrup

1. Combine strawberries and granulated sugar in small bowl; toss to coat. Set aside while preparing French toast.

2. Whisk eggs, milk, flour, vanilla and salt in shallow bowl or pie plate until well blended. Melt 1/2 tablespoon butter in large skillet over medium-high heat. Working with two slices at a time, dip bread into egg mixture, turning to coat completely; let excess drip off. Add to skillet; cook 3 to 4 minutes per side or until golden brown. Repeat with remaining butter and bread slices.

3. Top each serving with strawberry mixture and banana slices. Garnish with whipped cream and powdered sugar; serve with maple syrup.

Hearty Hash Brown Casserole

MAKES ABOUT 16 SERVINGS

2 cups sour cream

2 cups (8 ounces) shredded Colby cheese, divided

1 can (10¾ ounces) cream of chicken soup

½ cup (1 stick) butter, melted

1 small onion, finely chopped

¾ teaspoon salt

½ teaspoon black pepper

1 package (30 ounces) frozen shredded hash brown potatoes, thawed

1. Preheat oven to 375°F. Spray 13×9-inch baking dish with nonstick cooking spray.

2. Combine sour cream, 1½ cups cheese, soup, butter, onion, salt and pepper in large bowl; mix well. Add potatoes; stir until well blended. Spread mixture in prepared baking dish. (Do not pack down.) Sprinkle with remaining ½ cup cheese.

3. Bake 45 minutes or until cheese is melted and top of casserole is beginning to brown.

Breakfast Biscuit Bake

MAKES 8 SERVINGS

8 ounces bacon, chopped

1 small onion, finely chopped

1 clove garlic, minced

1/4 teaspoon red pepper flakes

5 eggs

1/4 cup milk

1/2 cup (2 ounces) shredded white Cheddar cheese, divided

1/4 teaspoon salt

1/8 teaspoon black pepper

1 package (16 ounces) refrigerated jumbo buttermilk biscuits (8 biscuits)

1. Preheat oven to 425°F. Cook bacon in large ovenproof skillet until crisp. Remove to paper towel-lined plate. Drain off and reserve drippings, leaving 1 tablespoon in skillet.

2. Add onion, garlic and red pepper flakes to skillet; cook and stir over medium heat about 8 minutes or until onion is softened. Set aside to cool slightly.

3. Whisk eggs, milk, 1/4 cup cheese, salt and black pepper in medium bowl until well blended. Stir in onion mixture.

4. Wipe out any onion mixture remaining in skillet; grease with additional drippings, if necessary. Separate biscuits and arrange in single layer in bottom of skillet. (Bottom of skillet should be completely covered.) Pour egg mixture over biscuits; sprinkle with remaining 1/4 cup cheese and cooked bacon.

5. Bake 25 minutes or until puffed and golden brown. Serve warm.

Chocolate Cherry Pancakes

MAKES ABOUT 6 SERVINGS

2	cups all-purpose flour	$1/2$	teaspoon baking soda
1	cup dried cherries	$1/2$	teaspoon salt
$2/3$	cup semisweet chocolate chips	$1^1/2$	cups milk
$1/3$	cup sugar	2	eggs
$4^1/2$	teaspoons baking powder	$1/4$	cup ($1/2$ stick) butter, melted

1. Combine flour, dried cherries, chocolate chips, sugar, baking powder, baking soda and salt in large bowl; mix well.

2. Whisk milk, eggs and butter in medium bowl until well blended Add to flour mixture; stir just until dry ingredients are moistened. (Add $1/4$ to $1/2$ cup additional milk if thinner pancakes are desired.)

3. Heat griddle or large nonstick skillet over medium heat until a drop of water sizzles when dropped on surface. Pour batter onto griddle $1/4$ cup at a time. Cook 2 to 3 minutes per side or until golden brown.

Apple Butter Spice Muffins

MAKES 12 MUFFINS

$1/2$ cup sugar

1 teaspoon ground cinnamon

$1/4$ teaspoon ground nutmeg

$1/8$ teaspoon ground allspice

$1/2$ cup chopped pecans or walnuts

2 cups all-purpose flour

2 teaspoons baking powder

$1/4$ teaspoon salt

1 cup milk

$1/4$ cup vegetable oil

1 egg

$1/4$ cup apple butter

1. Preheat oven to 400°F. Line 12 standard (2$1/2$-inch) muffin cups with paper baking cups or spray with nonstick cooking spray.

2. Combine sugar, cinnamon, nutmeg and allspice in large bowl. Remove 2 tablespoons sugar mixture to small bowl; toss with pecans until coated. Add flour, baking powder and salt to remaining sugar mixture; mix well.

3. Whisk milk, oil and egg in medium bowl until well blended. Add to flour mixture; stir just until dry ingredients are moistened. Spoon 1 tablespoon batter into each prepared muffin cup. Top with 1 teaspoon apple butter; spoon remaining batter evenly over apple butter. Sprinkle with pecan mixture.

4. Bake 20 to 25 minutes or until golden brown and toothpick inserted into centers comes out clean. Remove to wire rack to cool 10 minutes. Serve warm or cool completely.

Bacon and Potato Frittata

MAKES 4 TO 6 SERVINGS

5 eggs
½ cup bacon, crisp-cooked and crumbled
¼ cup half-and-half or milk
⅛ teaspoon salt

⅛ teaspoon black pepper
3 tablespoons butter
2 cups frozen O'Brien hash brown potatoes with onions and peppers

1. Preheat broiler. Whisk eggs in medium bowl. Add bacon, half-and-half, salt and pepper; whisk until well blended.

2. Melt butter in large broilerproof skillet over medium-high heat. Add potatoes; cook and stir 4 minutes.

3. Pour egg mixture into skillet. Reduce heat to medium; cover and cook 6 minutes or until eggs are set at edges (top will still be wet).

4. Transfer skillet to broiler. Broil 4 inches from heat source 1 to 2 minutes or until top of frittata is golden brown and center is set.

Blueberry-Orange French Toast Casserole

MAKES 6 SERVINGS

10 slices bread, cut into 1-inch cubes	½ cup sugar
3 tablespoons butter, melted	1 tablespoon grated orange peel
1½ cups milk	½ teaspoon vanilla
3 eggs	1½ cups fresh blueberries

1. Spray 8- or 9-inch square baking dish with nonstick cooking spray.

2. Combine bread cubes and butter in medium bowl; toss to coat.

3. Whisk milk, eggs, sugar, orange peel and vanilla in large bowl until well blended. Add bread cubes and blueberries; toss to coat. Pour into prepared baking dish; cover and refrigerate at least 8 hours or overnight.

4. Preheat oven to 325°F. Bake 1 hour or until bread is browned and center is set. Let stand 5 minutes before serving.

Crunchy Hash Brown Waffles

MAKES 4 WAFFLES (8 SERVINGS)

4 cups finely shredded potatoes
½ cup finely diced onion
1 egg
¼ cup all-purpose flour
2 tablespoons vegetable oil

1 teaspoon salt
Black pepper
Ketchup, sour cream and/or shredded Cheddar cheese (optional)

1. Preheat waffle maker to medium-high. Combine potatoes, onion, egg, flour, oil and salt in large bowl. Season with pepper; mix well.

2. Scoop 1 cup potato mixture onto waffle maker; carefully spread to cover surface. Close and cook about 8 minutes or until golden brown and crisp. Serve with desired toppings.

Note: Hash brown waffles can also be served as a side dish with roasted chicken or fish.

Cornmeal Pancakes

MAKES 4 SERVINGS

2 cups buttermilk
2 eggs, lightly beaten
$^1/_4$ cup sugar
2 tablespoons butter, melted
$1^1/_2$ cups yellow cornmeal

$^3/_4$ cup all-purpose flour
$1^1/_2$ teaspoons baking powder
1 teaspoon salt
Fresh blueberries (optional)
Additional butter (optional)

1. Whisk buttermilk, eggs, sugar and 2 tablespoons butter in large bowl until well blended.

2. Combine cornmeal, flour, baking powder and salt in medium bowl; mix well. Add to buttermilk mixture; stir just until blended. Let stand 5 minutes.

3. Lightly grease griddle or large skillet; heat over medium heat. Pour batter onto griddle $^1/_3$ cup at a time. Cook 3 minutes or until tops of pancakes are bubbly and appear dry; turn and cook 2 minutes or until bottoms are golden brown. Top with blueberries and additional butter, if desired.

Ham and Swiss Biscuits

MAKES ABOUT 18 BISCUITS

2   cups all-purpose flour

2   teaspoons baking powder

1/2   teaspoon baking soda

1/4   teaspoon salt

1/2   cup (1 stick) cold butter,
     cut into small pieces

2/3   cup buttermilk

1/2   cup (2 ounces) shredded
     Swiss cheese

2   ounces ham, finely chopped

1. Preheat oven to 450°F. Line baking sheet with parchment paper or spray with nonstick cooking spray.

2. Combine flour, baking powder, baking soda and salt in medium bowl; mix well. Cut in butter with pastry blender or two knives until mixture resembles coarse crumbs. Stir in buttermilk, 1 tablespoon at a time, until slightly sticky dough forms. Stir in cheese and ham.

3. Turn out dough onto lightly floured surface; knead lightly. Roll out dough to 1/2-inch thickness. Cut out biscuits with 2-inch round cutter. Place on prepared baking sheet.

4. Bake 10 minutes or until browned. Serve warm.

SOUPS

Creamy Tomato Soup

MAKES 6 SERVINGS

3 tablespoons olive oil, divided
2 tablespoons butter
1 large onion, finely chopped
2 cloves garlic, minced
2 teaspoons sugar
1 teaspoon salt
1/2 teaspoon dried oregano

2 cans (28 ounces each) peeled Italian plum tomatoes, undrained
4 cups 1/2-inch focaccia cubes (half of 9-ounce loaf)
1/2 teaspoon ground black pepper
1/2 cup whipping cream

1. Heat 2 tablespoons oil and butter in large saucepan or Dutch oven over medium-high heat. Add onion; cook and stir 5 minutes or until softened. Add garlic, sugar, salt and oregano; cook and stir 30 seconds. Stir in tomatoes with juice; bring to a boil. Reduce heat to medium-low; simmer 45 minutes, stirring occasionally.

2. Meanwhile, prepare croutons. Preheat oven to 350°F. Combine focaccia cubes, remaining 1 tablespoon oil and pepper in large bowl; toss to coat. Spread on large rimmed baking sheet. Bake 10 minutes or until bread cubes are golden brown.

3. Blend soup with hand-held immersion blender until smooth. (Or process soup in batches in food processor or blender.) Stir in cream; cook until heated through. Top with croutons.

Chicken Noodle Soup

MAKES 8 SERVINGS

2 tablespoons butter
1 cup chopped onion
1 cup sliced carrots
1/2 cup diced celery
2 tablespoons vegetable oil
1 pound chicken breast tenderloins
1 pound chicken thigh fillets

4 cups chicken broth, divided
2 cups water
1 tablespoon minced fresh parsley, plus additional for garnish
1 1/2 teaspoons salt
1/2 teaspoon black pepper
3 cups uncooked egg noodles

1. Melt butter in large saucepan or Dutch oven over medium-low heat. Add onion, carrots and celery; cook 8 minutes or until vegetables are soft, stirring occasionally.

2. Meanwhile, heat oil in large skillet over medium-high heat. Add chicken in single layer; cook 12 minutes or until lightly browned and cooked through, turning once. Remove chicken to large cutting board. Add 1 cup broth to skillet; cook 1 minute, scraping up browned bits from bottom of skillet. Add broth to vegetables in saucepan. Stir in remaining 3 cups broth, water, 1 tablespoon parsley, salt and pepper.

3. Chop chicken into 1-inch pieces when cool enough to handle. Add to soup; bring to a boil over medium-high heat. Reduce heat to medium-low; cook 15 minutes.

4. Stir in noodles; cook 15 minutes or until noodles are tender. Garnish with additional parsley.

Sausage Rice Soup

MAKES 4 TO 6 SERVINGS

2 teaspoons olive oil

8 ounces Italian sausage, casings removed

1 small onion, chopped

1/2 teaspoon fennel seeds

1 tablespoon tomato paste

4 cups chicken broth

1 can (about 14 ounces) whole tomatoes, undrained, crushed with hands or coarsely chopped

1 1/2 cups water

1/2 cup uncooked rice

1/4 teaspoon salt

1/8 teaspoon black pepper

2 to 3 ounces baby spinach

1/3 cup shredded mozzarella cheese (optional)

1. Heat oil in large saucepan or Dutch oven over medium-high heat. Add sausage; cook 8 minutes or until browned, stirring to break up meat. Add onion; cook and stir 5 minutes or until softened. Add fennel seeds; cook and stir 30 seconds. Add tomato paste; cook and stir 1 minute.

2. Stir in broth, tomatoes with juice, water, rice, 1/4 teaspoon salt and 1/8 teaspoon pepper; bring to a boil. Reduce heat to medium-low; cook 18 minutes or until rice is tender.

3. Stir in spinach; cook 3 minutes or until wilted. Season with additional salt and pepper. Sprinkle with cheese, if desired, just before serving.

Italian-Style Meatball Soup

MAKES 8 SERVINGS

8 ounces ground beef

4 ounces bulk Italian sausage

1 onion, finely chopped, divided

1/3 cup plain dry bread crumbs

1 egg

1/2 teaspoon salt

4 cups beef or vegetable broth

2 cups water

1 can (about 14 ounces) stewed tomatoes

1 can (8 ounces) pizza sauce

2 cups sliced cabbage

1 can (about 15 ounces) kidney beans, rinsed and drained

2 carrots, sliced

1/2 cup frozen Italian green beans

1. Combine beef, sausage, 2 tablespoons onion, bread crumbs, egg and salt in large bowl; stir until well blended. Shape into 32 (1-inch) meatballs.

2. Brown half of meatballs in large skillet over medium heat, turning frequently. Drain on paper towel-lined plate. Repeat with remaining meatballs.

3. Combine broth, water, tomatoes and pizza sauce in large saucepan or Dutch oven; bring to a boil over medium-high heat. Add meatballs, remaining onion, cabbage, beans and carrots; return to a boil. Reduce heat to medium-low; simmer 20 minutes.

4. Stir in green beans; cook 10 minutes or until vegetables are tender.

Broccoli Cheese Soup

MAKES 4 TO 6 SERVINGS

6 tablespoons (³/₄ stick) butter
1 cup chopped onion
1 clove garlic, minced
¼ cup all-purpose flour
2 cups vegetable broth
2 cups milk
1½ teaspoons Dijon mustard
½ teaspoon salt
¼ teaspoon ground nutmeg
¼ teaspoon black pepper

⅛ teaspoon hot pepper sauce
1 package (16 ounces) frozen broccoli (5 cups)
2 carrots, shredded (1 cup)
6 ounces pasteurized process cheese product, cubed
1 cup (4 ounces) shredded sharp Cheddar cheese, plus additional for garnish

1. Melt butter in large saucepan or Dutch oven over medium-low heat. Add onion; cook and stir 8 minutes or until softened. Add garlic; cook and stir 1 minute. Increase heat to medium. Whisk in flour until smooth; cook and stir 3 minutes without browning.

2. Gradually whisk in broth and milk. Add mustard, salt, nutmeg, black pepper and hot pepper sauce; cook 15 minutes or until thickened, stirring occasionally.

3. Add broccoli; cook 15 minutes. Add carrots; cook 10 minutes or until vegetables are tender.

4. Remove half of soup to food processor or blender; process until smooth. Return to saucepan. Add cheese product and 1 cup Cheddar; cook and stir over low heat until cheese is melted. Garnish soup with additional Cheddar.

Black Bean Soup

MAKES 4 TO 6 SERVINGS

2 tablespoons vegetable oil	2 tablespoons cider vinegar
1 cup diced onion	2 teaspoons chili powder
1 stalk celery, diced	½ teaspoon salt
2 carrots, diced	½ teaspoon ground red pepper
½ small green bell pepper, diced	½ teaspoon ground cumin
4 cloves garlic, minced	¼ teaspoon liquid smoke
4 cans (about 15 ounces each) black beans, rinsed and drained, divided	Optional toppings: sour cream, chopped green onions and/ or shredded Cheddar cheese
4 cups (32 ounces) chicken or vegetable broth, divided	

1. Heat oil in large saucepan or Dutch oven over medium-low heat. Add onion, celery, carrots, bell pepper and garlic; cook 10 minutes, stirring occasionally.

2. Combine half of beans and 1 cup broth in food processor or blender; process until smooth. Add to vegetables in saucepan.

3. Stir in remaining beans, 3 cups broth, vinegar, chili powder, salt, red pepper, cumin and liquid smoke; bring to a boil over high heat. Reduce heat to medium-low; cook 1 hour or until vegetables are tender and soup is thickened, stirring occasionally. Garnish as desired.

Chicken Enchilada Soup

MAKES 8 TO 10 SERVINGS

- **2 tablespoons vegetable oil, divided**
- **1¹/₂ pounds boneless skinless chicken breasts, cut into ¹/₂-inch pieces**
- **¹/₂ cup chopped onion**
- **2 cloves garlic, minced**
- **2 cans (about 14 ounces each) chicken broth**
- **3 cups water, divided**
- **1 cup masa harina**
- **1 package (16 ounces) pasteurized process cheese product, cubed**

- **1 can (10 ounces) mild red enchilada sauce**
- **1 teaspoon chili powder**
- **¹/₂ teaspoon salt**
- **¹/₂ teaspoon ground cumin**
- **1 large tomato, seeded and chopped**
- **Crispy tortilla strips***

If tortilla strips are not available, crumble tortilla chips into bite-size pieces.

1. Heat 1 tablespoon oil in large saucepan or Dutch oven over medium-high heat. Add chicken; cook and stir 10 minutes or until no longer pink. Transfer to medium bowl with slotted spoon; drain any excess liquid from saucepan.

2. Heat remaining 1 tablespoon oil in same saucepan over medium-high heat. Add onion and garlic; cook and stir 3 minutes or until softened. Stir in broth.

3. Whisk 2 cups water into masa harina in large bowl until smooth. Whisk mixture into broth in saucepan. Stir in remaining 1 cup water, cheese product, enchilada sauce, chili powder, salt and cumin; bring to a boil over high heat. Stir in chicken. Reduce heat to medium-low; cook 30 minutes, stirring frequently.

4. Top with tomato and tortilla strips just before serving.

Rustic Country Turkey Soup

MAKES 4 TO 6 SERVINGS

1 tablespoon olive oil	1 teaspoon dried thyme
1 cup chopped onion	1/2 teaspoon poultry seasoning
3/4 cup sliced carrots	1/4 teaspoon salt
4 ounces sliced mushrooms	1/8 teaspoon red pepper flakes
1 teaspoon minced garlic	2 cups chopped cooked turkey breast
2 cans (about 14 ounces each) chicken broth	1/4 cup chopped fresh parsley
2 ounces uncooked rotini pasta	

1. Heat oil in large saucepan or Dutch oven over medium-high heat. Add onion and carrots; cook and stir 2 minutes. Add mushrooms; cook 2 minutes. Add garlic; cook and stir 30 seconds. Stir in broth; bring to a boil.

2. Stir in pasta, thyme, poultry seasoning, salt and red pepper flakes; return to a boil. Reduce heat to low; cover and simmer 8 minutes or until pasta is tender.

3. Remove from heat; stir in turkey and parsley. Cover and let stand 5 minutes before serving.

Roasted Butternut Squash Soup

MAKES 4 SERVINGS

1 butternut squash (about 1½ pounds)

2 tablespoons olive oil

¾ teaspoon salt, divided

⅔ cup chopped onion

2½ cups vegetable broth

1 Granny Smith apple, peeled and cubed

¼ teaspoon ground cinnamon

⅛ teaspoon ground nutmeg

⅛ teaspoon black pepper

¼ cup half-and-half

Roasted pumpkin seeds (optional)

1. Preheat oven to 400°F. Line baking sheet with foil. Peel squash; cut in half lengthwise. Remove and discard seeds and strings. Cut squash into 2-inch cubes; place on prepared baking sheet. Drizzle with 1 tablespoon oil; sprinkle with ¼ teaspoon salt and toss to coat. Roast 12 minutes or until almost tender.

2. Meanwhile, heat remaining 1 tablespoon oil in large saucepan over medium heat. Add onion; cook and stir about 5 minutes or until soft and lightly browned. Add broth, apple and remaining ½ teaspoon salt; bring to a boil over high heat. Reduce heat to low; cover and simmer 10 minutes.

3. Add squash; cover and simmer 6 minutes or until tender. Remove from heat.

4. Working in batches, process soup in blender or food processor until smooth (or use handheld immersion blender). Return to saucepan; stir in cinnamon, nutmeg and pepper. Cook and stir over medium-low heat 3 minutes. Stir in half-and-half until blended. Sprinkle with pumpkin seeds, if desired.

Grandma's Minestrone

MAKES 4 SERVINGS

1 pound ground beef

1 package (16 ounces) frozen mixed vegetables

2 cans (8 ounces each) tomato sauce

1 can (about 15 ounces) red beans, rinsed and drained

1 can (about 14 ounces) diced tomatoes

1 can (about 14 ounces) beef broth

1/4 head shredded green cabbage (about 2 cups)

1 cup chopped onion

1 cup chopped celery

1/2 cup chopped fresh Italian parsley

1 tablespoon dried basil

1 tablespoon Italian seasoning

1 teaspoon salt

1 teaspoon black pepper

1 cup cooked macaroni

Slow Cooker Directions

1. Brown beef in large skillet over medium-high heat, stirring to break up meat. Drain fat. Transfer beef to slow cooker.

2. Stir in mixed vegetables, tomato sauce, beans, diced tomatoes, broth, cabbage, onion, celery, parsley, basil, Italian seasoning, salt and pepper. Cover; cook on LOW 6 to 8 hours.

3. Stir in macaroni. Cover; cook on HIGH 20 minutes.

Chicken, Barley and Vegetable Soup

MAKES 6 SERVINGS

8 ounces boneless skinless chicken breasts, cut into ½-inch pieces

8 ounces boneless skinless chicken thighs, cut into ½-inch pieces

1 teaspoon salt

¼ teaspoon black pepper

1 tablespoon olive oil

½ cup uncooked pearl barley

4 cans (about 14 ounces each) chicken broth

2 cups water

1 bay leaf

2 cups baby carrots

2 cups diced peeled potatoes

2 cups sliced mushrooms

2 cups frozen peas

3 tablespoons sour cream

1 tablespoon chopped fresh dill *or* 1 teaspoon dried dill weed

1. Sprinkle chicken with salt and pepper. Heat oil in large saucepan or Dutch oven over medium-high heat. Add chicken; cook without stirring 2 minutes or until golden brown. Turn chicken; cook 2 minutes. Remove to plate.

2. Add barley to saucepan; cook and stir 1 to 2 minutes or until barley begins to brown, adding 1 tablespoon broth, if necessary, to prevent burning. Add remaining broth, water and bay leaf; bring to a boil. Reduce heat to low; cover and simmer 30 minutes.

3. Add chicken, carrots, potatoes and mushrooms to saucepan; cook over medium heat 10 minutes or until vegetables are tender, stirring occasionally. Add peas; cook 2 minutes. Remove and discard bay leaf.

4. Top with sour cream and dill; serve immediately.

•SALADS•

Country Time Macaroni Salad

MAKES 4 TO 6 SERVINGS

1 cup uncooked elbow macaroni	³/₄ teaspoon salt
¹/₃ cup mayonnaise	1 cup thawed frozen green peas
¹/₄ cup plain yogurt	1 cup chopped green bell pepper
4 teaspoons sweet pickle relish	²/₃ cup thinly sliced celery
1¹/₂ teaspoons dried dill weed	8 ounces ham, cubed
1 teaspoon prepared yellow mustard	¹/₂ cup (2 ounces) shredded Cheddar cheese, divided

1. Cook pasta according to package directions; drain and rinse under cold water until cool.

2. Meanwhile, whisk mayonnaise, yogurt, pickle relish, dill weed, mustard and salt in small bowl until well blended.

3. Combine peas, bell pepper, celery and ham in medium bowl.

4. Add pasta and mayonnaise mixture to pea mixture; stir to blend. Stir in half of cheese; toss gently to combine. Sprinkle with remaining cheese. Serve immediately.

Chinese Chicken Salad

MAKES 4 TO 6 SERVINGS

3 tablespoons peanut or vegetable oil

3 tablespoons rice vinegar

2 tablespoons soy sauce

1 tablespoon honey

1 teaspoon minced fresh ginger

1 teaspoon dark sesame oil

1 clove garlic, minced

¼ teaspoon red pepper flakes (optional)

4 cups shredded cooked chicken or turkey

4 cups packed shredded napa cabbage or romaine lettuce

1 cup shredded carrots

½ cup thinly sliced green onions

1 package (3 ounces) ramen noodles, crumbled* or 1 can (5 ounces) chow mein noodles

¼ cup chopped cashew nuts or peanuts (optional)

*Use any flavor; discard seasoning packet.

1. For dressing, combine peanut oil, vinegar, soy sauce, honey, ginger, sesame oil, garlic and red pepper flakes, if desired, in small jar with tight-fitting lid; shake until well blended.

2. Place chicken in large bowl. Pour dressing over chicken; toss to coat.**

3. Add cabbage, carrots, green onions and crumbled noodles to bowl with chicken; toss to coat. Sprinkle with cashews, if desired.

**Salad may be made ahead to this point; cover and refrigerate chicken mixture until ready to serve.

Warm Potato Salad

MAKES 6 TO 8 SERVINGS

2 pounds fingerling potatoes, unpeeled

3 slices thick-cut bacon, cut into $1/2$-inch pieces

1 small onion, diced

2 tablespoons olive oil

$1/4$ cup cider vinegar

2 tablespoons capers, drained

1 tablespoon Dijon mustard

$3/4$ teaspoon salt

$1/4$ teaspoon black pepper

$1/3$ cup chopped fresh parsley

1. Place potatoes in large saucepan; add cold water to cover by 2 inches. Bring to a boil over high heat. Reduce heat to medium; cook 10 to 12 minutes or just until potatoes are tender when pierced with tip of small knife.

2. Drain potatoes; let stand until cool enough to handle. Meanwhile, dry out saucepan with paper towels. Add bacon to saucepan; cook until crisp, stirring occasionally. Remove to paper-lined plate with slotted spoon. Drain off all but 1 tablespoon drippings.

3. Add onion and oil to saucepan; cook 10 minutes or until onion begins to turn golden, stirring occasionally. Cut potatoes crosswise into $1/2$-inch slices.

4. Add vinegar, capers, mustard, salt and pepper to saucepan; mix well. Remove from heat; stir in potatoes. Add parsley and bacon; stir gently to coat.

Southwestern Salad

MAKES 6 SERVINGS

1 can (about 15 ounces) black beans, rinsed and drained

1½ cups cooked corn

1½ cups chopped seeded tomatoes

½ cup thinly sliced green onions

¼ cup minced fresh cilantro

½ cup vegetable oil

2 tablespoons red wine vinegar

1 teaspoon salt

½ teaspoon black pepper

1. Combine beans, corn, tomatoes, green onions and cilantro in large bowl; mix well.

2. Whisk oil, vinegar, salt and pepper in small bowl until well blended.

3. Pour dressing over salad; stir gently to coat. Serve at room temperature or slightly chilled.

Coleslaw

MAKES 10 SERVINGS

1 medium head green cabbage, shredded

1 medium carrot, shredded

½ cup mayonnaise

½ cup milk

⅓ cup sugar

3 tablespoons lemon juice

1½ tablespoons white vinegar

1 teaspoon salt

⅛ teaspoon black pepper

1. Combine cabbage and carrot in large bowl; mix well.

2. Whisk mayonnaise, milk, sugar, lemon juice, vinegar, salt and pepper in medium bowl until well blended.

3. Add dressing to cabbage mixture; stir until blended.

SOUTHWESTERN SALAD

Thai-Style Warm Noodle Salad

MAKES 4 SERVINGS

8 ounces uncooked angel hair pasta

½ cup chunky peanut butter

¼ cup soy sauce

¼ teaspoon red pepper flakes

2 green onions, thinly sliced

1 carrot, shredded

1. Cook pasta according to package directions.

2. Meanwhile, whisk peanut butter, soy sauce and red pepper flakes in large bowl until smooth.

3. Drain pasta, reserving 5 tablespoons cooking water. Whisk hot pasta water into peanut butter mixture until smooth.

4. Add pasta to sauce; toss to coat. Stir in green onions and carrot. Serve warm or at room temperature.

Notes: This salad can be prepared a day ahead and served warm or cold—perfect for potlucks, picnics and even lunch boxes. Add leftover cooked chicken, beef, pork or tofu to turn it into a heartier meal.

Mediterranean Chickpea Ramen Salad

MAKES 6 TO 8 SERVINGS

2 packages (3 ounces each) ramen noodles, broken into small pieces*

Juice of 1 lemon

3 tablespoons extra virgin olive oil

1 teaspoon coarse salt

$1/2$ teaspoon black pepper

1 can (about 15 ounces) chickpeas, rinsed and drained

2 tomatoes, diced

$3/4$ cup crumbled feta cheese

$1/2$ cup diced red onion

$1/2$ English cucumber, seeded and diced

$1/4$ cup finely chopped fresh Italian parsley

*Use any flavor; discard seasoning packets.

1. Cook noodles according to package directions; drain well.

2. Whisk lemon juice, oil, salt and pepper in large bowl until well blended.

3. Add chickpeas, tomatoes, cheese, onion, cucumber, parsley and noodles; toss to coat.

Sweet and Sour Broccoli Pasta Salad

MAKES 4 TO 6 SERVINGS

8 ounces uncooked cellentani or rotini pasta

2 cups broccoli florets

1 medium Red or Golden Delicious apple, chopped

²/₃ cup shredded carrots

¹/₃ cup plain yogurt

¹/₃ cup apple juice

3 tablespoons cider vinegar

2 tablespoons olive oil

1 tablespoon Dijon mustard

1 teaspoon salt

1 teaspoon honey

¹/₂ teaspoon dried thyme

1. Cook pasta according to package directions, adding broccoli during last 2 minutes of cooking. Drain pasta and broccoli; rinse under cold water until cool.

2. Combine pasta, broccoli, apple and carrots in medium bowl; stir to blend.

3. Whisk yogurt, apple juice, vinegar, oil, mustard, salt, honey and thyme in small bowl until well blended.

4. Pour dressing over pasta mixture; toss to coat.

Chicken Satay Salad

MAKES 4 SERVINGS

1/4 **cup plus 2 tablespoons peanut sauce, divided**

2 **tablespoons lime juice**

1 **tablespoon unseasoned rice vinegar**

3 **teaspoons toasted sesame oil, divided**

1 **pound chicken tenders, cut in half lengthwise**

4 **cups chopped romaine lettuce**

1 **red bell pepper, thinly sliced**

1 **cup shredded carrots**

1 **cup sliced Persian cucumbers***

1/4 **cup chopped fresh cilantro**

1 **tablespoon peanuts, chopped**

*Persian cucumbers are similar to English cucumbers; they have fewer seeds and contain less water than traditional cucumbers, which gives them a sweeter flavor and crunchier texture.

1. Whisk 1/4 cup peanut sauce, lime juice, vinegar and 1 teaspoon oil in large bowl until smooth and well blended.

2. Heat remaining 2 teaspoons oil in large nonstick skillet over medium-high heat. Add chicken; cook and stir 4 minutes or until no longer pink. Remove from heat. Add remaining 2 tablespoons peanut sauce; gently toss to coat evenly.

3. Add lettuce, bell pepper, carrots and cucumbers to dressing in large bowl; toss to coat.

4. Divide salad evenly among four plates; top with chicken, cilantro and peanuts.

Garden Vegetable Pasta Salad with Bacon

MAKES 6 TO 8 SERVINGS

12 ounces uncooked rotini pasta

2 cups broccoli florets

1 can (about 14 ounces) diced tomatoes

2 medium carrots, diagonally sliced

2 stalks celery, sliced

10 medium mushrooms, thinly sliced

½ medium red onion, thinly sliced

8 ounces bacon, crisp-cooked and crumbled

1 bottle (8 ounces) Italian or ranch salad dressing

½ cup (2 ounces) shredded Cheddar cheese

1 tablespoon dried parsley flakes

2 teaspoons dried basil

¼ teaspoon black pepper

1. Cook pasta according to package directions; drain and rinse under cold water until cool.

2. Combine broccoli, tomatoes, carrots, celery, mushrooms and onion in large bowl. Add pasta and bacon; toss gently to blend.

3. Add salad dressing, cheese, parsley, basil and pepper; toss gently to coat.

Fruit Salad with Creamy Banana Dressing

MAKES 8 SERVINGS

2 cups fresh pineapple chunks
1 cup cantaloupe cubes
1 cup honeydew melon cubes
1 cup fresh blackberries
1 cup sliced fresh strawberries
1 cup seedless red grapes

1 medium apple, diced
2 medium ripe bananas, sliced
½ cup vanilla Greek yogurt
2 tablespoons honey
1 tablespoon lemon juice
¼ teaspoon ground nutmeg

1. Combine pineapple, cantaloupe, honeydew, blackberries, strawberries, grapes and apple in large bowl; mix gently.

2. Combine bananas, yogurt, honey, lemon juice and nutmeg in blender or food processor; blend until smooth.

3. Pour dressing over fruit mixture; toss gently to coat. Serve immediately.

CHICKEN & TURKEY

Crispy Ranch Chicken

MAKES 6 SERVINGS

1½ cups cornflake crumbs	½ teaspoon black pepper
1 teaspoon dried rosemary	1½ cups ranch salad dressing
½ teaspoon salt	3 pounds bone-in chicken pieces

1. Preheat oven to 375°F. Spray 13×9-inch baking dish with nonstick cooking spray. Combine cornflake crumbs, rosemary, salt and pepper in medium bowl; mix well.

2. Pour salad dressing in separate medium bowl. Dip chicken pieces in salad dressing; turn to coat all sides. Roll chicken in crumb mixture to coat. Place in prepared baking dish.

3. Bake 50 to 55 minutes or until cooked through (165°F).

Variation: To add Italian flavor to this dish, substitute 1¼ cups Italian-seasoned dry bread crumbs and ¼ cup grated Parmesan cheese for the cornflake crumbs, rosemary, salt and pepper. Prepare recipe as directed.

Southwest Turkey Bake

MAKES 8 SERVINGS

1 pound ground turkey

1 can (about 15 ounces) black beans, rinsed and drained

1 cup salsa

$\frac{1}{2}$ teaspoon ground cumin

$\frac{1}{8}$ teaspoon ground red pepper

1 package ($8\frac{1}{2}$ ounces) corn muffin mix

$\frac{3}{4}$ cup chicken broth

1 egg

$\frac{3}{4}$ cup (3 ounces) shredded Mexican cheese blend

Lime wedges (optional)

1. Preheat oven to 400°F. Cook turkey in large nonstick skillet over medium-high heat 6 to 8 minutes or until no longer pink, stirring to break up meat.

2. Add beans, salsa, cumin and red pepper; cook and stir 2 minutes. Spoon into 13×9-inch baking dish.

3. Combine corn muffin mix, broth and egg in medium bowl; mix well. Spread batter over turkey mixture; sprinkle with cheese.

4. Bake 15 minutes or until edges of topping are lightly browned. Serve with lime wedges, if desired.

Chicken Scarpiello

MAKES 6 SERVINGS

3   tablespoons extra virgin olive oil, divided

1   pound spicy Italian sausage, cut into 1-inch pieces

1   whole chicken (about 3 pounds), cut into 10 pieces*

1   teaspoon salt, divided

1   large onion, chopped

2   red, yellow or orange bell peppers, cut into $1/4$-inch strips

3   cloves garlic, minced

$1/2$ cup dry white wine (such as sauvignon blanc)

$1/2$ cup chicken broth

$1/2$ cup coarsely chopped seeded hot cherry peppers

$1/2$ cup liquid from cherry pepper jar

1   teaspoon dried oregano

$1/4$ cup chopped fresh Italian parsley

*Or, purchase 2 bone-in chicken leg quarters and 2 chicken breasts; separate drumsticks and thighs and cut breasts in half.

1. Heat 1 tablespoon oil in large skillet over medium-high heat. Add sausage; cook about 10 minutes or until well browned on all sides, stirring occasionally. Remove to plate.

2. Heat 1 tablespoon oil in same skillet. Sprinkle chicken with $1/2$ teaspoon salt; arrange skin side down in single layer in skillet (cook in batches, if necessary). Cook about 6 minutes per side or until browned. Remove to plate. Drain fat from skillet.

3. Heat remaining 1 tablespoon oil in skillet. Add onion and $1/2$ teaspoon salt; cook and stir 2 minutes or until softened, scraping up browned bits from bottom of skillet. Add bell peppers and garlic; cook and stir 5 minutes. Stir in wine; cook until liquid is reduced by half. Stir in broth, cherry peppers, cherry pepper liquid and oregano. Season with additional salt and black pepper; bring to a simmer.

4. Return sausage and chicken to skillet. Partially cover skillet; cook 10 minutes. Uncover; cook 15 minutes or until chicken is cooked through (165°F). Sprinkle with parsley.

Tip: If too much liquid remains in the skillet when the chicken is cooked through, remove the chicken and sausage and continue simmering the sauce to reduce it slightly.

Split-Biscuit Chicken Pie

MAKES 4 TO 5 SERVINGS

⅓ **cup butter**	½ **teaspoon black pepper**
⅓ **cup all-purpose flour**	4 **cups diced cooked chicken**
2½ **cups whole milk**	2 **jars (4 ounces each) diced pimientos**
1 **tablespoon chicken bouillon granules**	1 **cup frozen green peas, thawed**
½ **teaspoon dried thyme**	1 **package (6 ounces) refrigerated biscuits**

1. Preheat oven to 350°F. Spray 2-quart casserole or 12×8-inch baking dish with nonstick cooking spray.

2. Melt butter in large skillet over medium heat. Add flour; whisk until well blended. Add milk, bouillon, thyme and pepper; whisk until smooth. Cook and stir until thickened. Remove from heat; stir in chicken, pimientos and peas. Pour mixture into prepared casserole.

3. Bake 30 minutes. Meanwhile, bake biscuits according to package directions.

4. Split biscuits in half; arrange cut sides down over chicken mixture. Bake 3 minutes or until biscuits are heated through.

Turkey Vegetable Chili Mac

MAKES 6 SERVINGS

1 tablespoon vegetable oil

12 ounces ground turkey

½ cup chopped onion

2 cloves garlic, minced

1 can (about 15 ounces) black beans, rinsed and drained

1 can (about 14 ounces) Mexican-style stewed tomatoes, undrained

1 can (about 14 ounces) diced tomatoes

1 cup frozen corn

1 teaspoon salt

1 teaspoon Mexican seasoning

½ cup uncooked elbow macaroni

⅓ cup sour cream

Finely chopped fresh cilantro or green onions (optional)

1. Heat oil in large saucepan over medium heat. Add turkey, onion and garlic; cook and stir 5 minutes or until turkey is no longer pink.

2. Stir in beans, tomatoes with juice, corn, salt and Mexican seasoning; bring to a boil over high heat. Reduce heat to low; cover and simmer 15 minutes, stirring occasionally.

3. Meanwhile, cook pasta according to package directions. Drain pasta; stir into turkey mixture. Cook, uncovered, 2 to 3 minutes or until heated through.

4. Top each serving with dollop of sour cream and cilantro, if desired.

Barbecue Chicken Pizza

MAKES 4 SERVINGS

1   package (16 ounces) refrigerated pizza dough

1   tablespoon olive oil

6   ounces boneless skinless chicken breasts, cut into strips (about 2×$\frac{1}{4}$ inch)

$\frac{1}{4}$ teaspoon salt

$\frac{1}{8}$ teaspoon black pepper

6   tablespoons barbecue sauce, divided

$\frac{2}{3}$ cup shredded mozzarella cheese, divided

$\frac{1}{2}$ cup shredded smoked Gouda cheese, divided

$\frac{1}{2}$ small red onion, cut vertically into $\frac{1}{8}$-inch slices

2   tablespoons chopped fresh cilantro

1. Preheat oven to 450°F. Line baking sheet with parchment paper. Let dough come to room temperature.

2. Heat oil in large skillet over medium-high heat. Season chicken with salt and pepper; cook 5 minutes or just until cooked though, stirring occasionally. Remove chicken to medium bowl. Add 2 tablespoons barbecue sauce; stir to coat.

3. Roll out dough into 12-inch circle on lightly floured surface. Transfer to prepared baking sheet. Spread remaining 4 tablespoons barbecue sauce over dough, leaving $\frac{1}{2}$-inch border. Sprinkle with 2 tablespoons mozzarella and 2 tablespoons Gouda. Top with chicken and onion; sprinkle with remaining cheeses.

4. Bake 12 to 15 minutes or until crust is browned and cheese is bubbly. Sprinkle with cilantro.

Cajun Chicken and Rice

MAKES 6 SERVINGS

4 chicken drumsticks, skin removed

4 chicken thighs, skin removed

2 teaspoons Cajun seasoning

¾ teaspoon salt

2 tablespoons vegetable oil

1 can (about 14 ounces) chicken broth

1 cup uncooked rice

1 medium green bell pepper, coarsely chopped

1 medium red bell pepper, coarsely chopped

½ cup finely chopped green onions

2 cloves garlic, minced

½ teaspoon dried thyme

¼ teaspoon ground turmeric

1. Preheat oven to 350°F. Spray 13×9-inch baking dish with nonstick cooking spray.

2. Pat chicken dry; sprinkle both sides with Cajun seasoning and salt. Heat oil in large skillet over medium-high heat. Add chicken; cook 4 to 5 minutes per side or until browned. Remove to plate.

3. Add broth to skillet; bring to a boil, scraping up browned bits from bottom of skillet. Add rice, bell peppers, green onions, garlic, thyme and turmeric; mix well. Spoon into prepared baking dish; top with chicken.

4. Cover and bake 1 hour or until chicken is cooked through (165°F).

Variation: For a one-dish meal, use an ovenproof skillet instead of a baking dish. Place the browned chicken on top of the rice mixture in the skillet, then cover and bake as directed.

Skillet Lasagna with Vegetables

MAKES 6 SERVINGS

- 8 ounces hot Italian turkey sausage, casings removed
- 8 ounces ground turkey
- 2 stalks celery, sliced
- 1/3 cup chopped onion
- 2 cups marinara sauce
- 1 1/3 cups water
- 4 ounces uncooked bowtie (farfalle) pasta

- 1 medium zucchini, halved lengthwise, then cut crosswise into 1/2-inch slices
- 3/4 cup chopped green or yellow bell pepper
- 1/2 cup (2 ounces) shredded mozzarella cheese
- 1/2 cup ricotta cheese
- 2 tablespoons finely grated Parmesan cheese

1. Heat large skillet over medium-high heat. Add sausage, ground turkey, celery and onion; cook and stir 6 to 8 minutes or until turkey is no longer pink.

2. Stir in marinara sauce and water; bring to a boil. Stir in pasta; mix well. Reduce heat to medium-low; cover and simmer 12 minutes.

3. Stir in zucchini and bell pepper; cover and cook 2 minutes. Uncover; cook 4 to 6 minutes or until vegetables are crisp-tender.

4. Sprinkle with mozzarella. Combine ricotta and Parmesan in small bowl; mix well. Drop by rounded teaspoonfuls over pasta mixture in skillet. Remove from heat; cover and let stand 10 minutes.

Sheet Pan Chicken and Sausage Supper

MAKES ABOUT 6 SERVINGS

1/3 cup olive oil

2 tablespoons balsamic vinegar

1 teaspoon salt

1 teaspoon garlic powder

1/2 teaspoon black pepper

1/4 teaspoon red pepper flakes

3 pounds bone-in chicken thighs and drumsticks

1 pound uncooked sweet Italian sausage (4 to 5 links), cut diagonally into 2-inch pieces

6 to 8 small red onions (about 1 1/2 pounds), each cut into 6 wedges

3 1/2 cups broccoli florets

1. Preheat oven to 425°F. Line baking sheet with foil, if desired.

2. Whisk oil, vinegar, salt, garlic powder, black pepper and red pepper flakes in small bowl until well blended. Combine chicken, sausage and onions on prepared baking sheet. Drizzle with oil mixture; toss until well coated. Spread meat and onions in single layer (chicken thighs should be skin side up).

3. Bake 30 minutes. Add broccoli to baking sheet; stir to coat broccoli with pan juices and turn sausage. Bake 30 minutes or until broccoli is beginning to brown and chicken is cooked through (165°F).

Pulled Chicken Sandwiches

MAKES 4 SERVINGS

1 cup water

1 cup barbecue sauce, divided

2 tablespoons Worcestershire sauce

2 pounds boneless skinless chicken thighs

1 small red onion, cut in half and thinly sliced

4 pretzel rolls or sandwich buns, split

$1/2$ cup cabbage slaw

1. Combine water, $3/4$ cup barbecue sauce and Worcestershire sauce in large saucepan; mix well. Add chicken and onion; stir to blend. (Liquid should just cover chicken; add additional water if necessary.) Bring to a simmer over medium-high heat.

2. Reduce heat to medium-low; cover and cook 35 minutes. Remove chicken to medium bowl; let stand 10 to 15 minutes or until cool enough to handle. Meanwhile, increase heat to medium-high; cook liquid in saucepan 10 to 15 minutes or until reduced by half.

3. Shred chicken into bite-size pieces in bowl. Add remaining $1/4$ cup barbecue sauce and $1/4$ cup reduced cooking liquid; toss to coat. (Serve remaining cooking liquid for dipping, if desired.)

4. Serve chicken mixture on rolls with cabbage slaw.

Turkey Vegetable Meatballs

MAKES 4 TO 6 SERVINGS

1 **pound ground turkey**	2 **cloves garlic, minced**
$\frac{1}{2}$ **cup finely chopped green onions**	$\frac{3}{4}$ **teaspoon salt**
$\frac{1}{2}$ **cup finely chopped green bell pepper**	$\frac{1}{2}$ **teaspoon Italian seasoning**
$\frac{1}{3}$ **cup old-fashioned oats**	$\frac{1}{4}$ **teaspoon fennel seeds**
$\frac{1}{4}$ **cup shredded carrot**	$\frac{1}{8}$ **teaspoon red pepper flakes (optional)**
$\frac{1}{4}$ **cup grated Parmesan cheese**	1 **tablespoon olive oil**
1 **egg**	**Marinara sauce, heated (optional)**

1. Combine turkey, green onions, bell pepper, oats, carrot, cheese, egg, garlic, salt, Italian seasoning, fennel seeds and red pepper flakes, if desired, in large bowl; mix well. Shape into 36 (1-inch) balls.

2. Heat oil in large nonstick skillet over medium-high heat. Add meatballs; cook 10 to 12 minutes or until no longer pink in center, turning frequently. (Use fork and spoon for easy turning.) Serve immediately with marinara sauce, if desired, or cool and freeze.*

*To freeze, cool completely and place in gallon-size resealable food storage bag. Release any excess air from bag and seal. Freeze bag flat for easier storage and faster thawing. This will also allow you to remove as many meatballs as needed without them sticking together. To reheat, place meatballs in a 12×8-inch microwavable dish and cook on HIGH 20 to 30 seconds or until hot.

Simple Roasted Chicken

MAKES 4 SERVINGS

1 whole chicken (about 4 pounds)
3 tablespoons butter, softened
1½ teaspoons salt
1 teaspoon onion powder
1 teaspoon dried thyme

½ teaspoon garlic powder
½ teaspoon paprika
½ teaspoon black pepper
Fresh parsley sprigs and lemon wedges (optional)

1. Preheat oven to 425°F. Pat chicken dry; place in small baking dish or on baking sheet.

2. Combine butter, salt, onion powder, thyme, garlic powder, paprika and pepper in small microwavable bowl; mash with fork until well blended. Loosen skin on breasts and thighs; spread about one third of butter mixture under skin.

3. Microwave remaining butter mixture until melted. Brush melted butter mixture all over outside of chicken and inside cavity. Tie drumsticks together with kitchen string and tuck wing tips under.

4. Roast 20 minutes. *Reduce oven temperature to 375°F.* Roast 45 to 55 minutes or until chicken is cooked through (165°F), basting once with pan juices during last 10 minutes of cooking time. Remove chicken to cutting board; tent with foil. Let stand 15 minutes before carving. Garnish with parsley and lemon wedges.

Chicken Enchilada Casserole

MAKES 8 SERVINGS

1 tablespoon olive oil

1 cup chopped red onion

1 can (4 ounces) diced green chiles

2 cans (10 ounces each) mild enchilada sauce

12 ounces shredded cooked chicken breast

$2/3$ cup sliced green onions

12 (6-inch) corn tortillas

$3/4$ cup (3 ounces) shredded Mexican cheese blend

$1/2$ cup sour cream (optional)

1. Preheat oven to 350°F. Spray $2^1/_2$-quart baking dish with nonstick cooking spray.

2. Heat oil in large skillet over medium-high heat. Add red onion and chiles; cook and stir 4 minutes or until onion is tender. Stir in enchilada sauce, chicken and green onions.

3. Place four tortillas in bottom of prepared baking dish. Top with 2 cups chicken mixture and $1/4$ cup cheese. Top with four tortillas, 1 cup chicken mixture and $1/4$ cup cheese, then remaining four tortillas, chicken mixture and cheese.

4. Cover and bake 20 minutes. Uncover; bake 10 minutes or until heated through. Let stand 10 minutes before serving. Serve with sour cream, if desired.

Chicken Parmesan Sliders

MAKES 12 SLIDERS

4 boneless skinless chicken breasts (6 to 8 ounces each)

1/4 cup all-purpose flour

2 eggs

1 tablespoon water

1 cup Italian-seasoned dry bread crumbs

1/2 cup grated Parmesan cheese

Salt and black pepper

Olive oil

12 slider buns (about 3 inches), split

3/4 cup marinara sauce

6 tablespoons Alfredo sauce

6 slices mozzarella cheese, cut into halves

2 tablespoons butter, melted

1/4 teaspoon garlic powder

6 tablespoons pesto sauce

1. Preheat oven to 375°F. Line baking sheet with foil; top with wire rack.

2. Pound chicken to 1/2-inch thickness between two sheets of waxed paper or plastic wrap with meat mallet or rolling pin. Cut each chicken breast crosswise into three pieces about the size of slider buns.

3. Place flour in shallow dish. Beat eggs and water in second shallow dish. Combine bread crumbs and Parmesan in third shallow dish. Season flour and egg mixtures with pinch of salt and pepper. Coat chicken pieces lightly with flour, shaking off excess. Dip in egg mixture, coating completely; roll in bread crumb mixture to coat. Place on large plate; let stand 10 minutes.

4. Heat 1/4 inch oil in large nonstick skillet over medium-high heat. Add chicken in single layer (cook in two batches if necessary); cook 3 to 4 minutes per side or until golden brown. Remove chicken to wire rack; bake 5 minutes or until cooked through (165°F). Remove rack with chicken from baking sheet.

5. Place slider buns on baking sheet with bottoms cut sides up and tops cut sides down. Spread 1 tablespoon marinara sauce over each bottom bun; top with piece of chicken. Spread 1/2 tablespoon Alfredo sauce over chicken; top with half slice of mozzarella. Combine butter and garlic powder in small bowl; brush mixture over top buns.

6. Bake 3 to 4 minutes or until mozzarella is melted and top buns are lightly toasted. Spread 1/2 tablespoon pesto over mozzarella; cover with top buns.

BEEF & PORK

Simple Shredded Pork Tacos

MAKES 6 SERVINGS

2 pounds boneless pork roast

1 cup salsa

1 can (4 ounces) diced green chiles

½ teaspoon garlic salt

½ teaspoon black pepper

Corn or flour tortillas (6-inch size), warmed

Optional toppings: tomatillo salsa, sliced jalapeño peppers, sour cream, shredded cheese and/or shredded lettuce

Slow Cooker Directions

1. Place pork in bottom of slow cooker. Combine salsa, chiles, garlic salt and pepper in small bowl; mix well. Pour salsa mixture over pork.

2. Cover; cook on LOW 8 hours. Remove pork to cutting board; shred with two forks.

3. Stir shredded pork back into slow cooker to keep warm. Serve with tortillas and desired toppings.

Meatloaf

MAKES 6 TO 8 SERVINGS

1 tablespoon vegetable oil	1 pound ground beef
2 green onions, minced	1 pound ground pork
1/4 cup minced green bell pepper	1 cup plain dry bread crumbs
1/4 cup grated carrot	2 teaspoons salt
3 cloves garlic, minced	1/2 teaspoon onion powder
3/4 cup milk	1/2 teaspoon black pepper
2 eggs, beaten	1/2 cup ketchup, divided

1. Preheat oven to 350°F.

2. Heat oil in large skillet over medium-high heat. Add green onions, bell pepper, carrot and garlic; cook and stir 5 minutes or until vegetables are softened.

3. Whisk milk and eggs in medium bowl until well blended. Gently mix beef, pork, bread crumbs, salt, onion powder and black pepper in large bowl with hands. Add milk mixture, vegetables and 1/4 cup ketchup; mix gently. Press into 9×5-inch loaf pan; place pan on rimmed baking sheet.

4. Bake 30 minutes. Spread remaining 1/4 cup ketchup over meatloaf; bake 1 hour or until cooked through (160°F). Cool in pan 10 minutes before slicing.

Little Italy Baked Ziti

MAKES 6 TO 8 SERVINGS

1 package (16 ounces) uncooked ziti pasta

1 pound bulk mild Italian sausage

3 cloves garlic, minced

3/4 cup dry white wine

1 jar (24 ounces) marinara sauce

1 can (about 14 ounces) diced tomatoes

2 tablespoons butter

2 cups (8 ounces) shredded mozzarella cheese, divided

1/2 cup coarsely chopped fresh basil, plus additional for garnish

1/4 cup grated Parmesan cheese

1. Cook pasta in large saucepan of salted boiling water according to package directions until al dente. Drain and return to saucepan; cover to keep warm.

2. Meanwhile, cook sausage in large skillet over medium-high heat about 8 minutes or until no longer pink, stirring to break up meat. Add garlic; cook and stir 1 minute. Add wine; cook 4 minutes or until almost evaporated.

3. Stir in marinara sauce, tomatoes and butter; bring to a boil. Reduce heat to medium-low; cook 20 minutes, stirring occasionally.

4. Preheat broiler. Spray 3-quart or 13×9-inch broilerproof baking dish with nonstick cooking spray.

5. Add sauce mixture, 1 cup mozzarella and 1/2 cup basil to pasta in saucepan; stir gently to coat. Spread in prepared baking dish; sprinkle with remaining 1 cup mozzarella and Parmesan.

6. Broil 2 to 3 minutes or until cheese begins to bubble and turn golden brown. Garnish with additional basil.

Southwestern Sloppy Joes

MAKES 8 SERVINGS

1 pound ground beef
1 cup chopped onion
¼ cup chopped celery
1 can (10 ounces) diced tomatoes with green chiles
1 can (8 ounces) tomato sauce
¼ cup water

4 teaspoons packed brown sugar
¾ teaspoon salt
½ teaspoon ground cumin
8 whole wheat hamburger buns, split

1. Cook beef, onion and celery in large skillet over medium-high heat 6 to 8 minutes or until meat begins to brown, stirring to break up meat. Drain fat.

2. Stir in tomatoes, tomato sauce, water, brown sugar, salt and cumin; bring to a boil over high heat. Reduce heat to low; simmer 20 minutes or until mixture thickens.

3. Spoon heaping ⅓ cup meat mixture onto each bun.

Pork Chop and Stuffing Skillet

MAKES 4 SERVINGS

4 thin bone-in pork chops (about 4 ounces each)

$\frac{1}{2}$ teaspoon salt

$\frac{1}{4}$ teaspoon dried thyme

$\frac{1}{4}$ teaspoon paprika

1 tablespoon olive oil

4 ounces bulk pork sausage

2 cups cornbread stuffing mix

$1\frac{1}{4}$ cups water

1 cup diced green bell pepper

$\frac{1}{4}$ teaspoon poultry seasoning

1. Preheat oven to 350°F. Sprinkle one side of pork chops with salt, thyme and paprika.

2. Heat oil in large ovenproof skillet over medium-high heat. Add pork chops, seasoned side down; cook 2 minutes. Remove to plate; tent with foil to keep warm.

3. Add sausage to skillet; cook 6 to 8 minutes or until no longer pink, stirring to break up meat. Remove from heat; stir in stuffing mix, water, bell pepper and poultry seasoning until blended. Arrange pork chops, seasoned side up, over stuffing mixture.

4. Cover and bake 15 minutes or until pork is barely pink in center. Let stand 5 minutes before serving.

French Dip Sandwiches

MAKES 6 SERVINGS

3 pounds boneless beef chuck roast

$1/2$ teaspoon salt

$1/2$ teaspoon black pepper

1 tablespoon olive oil

2 large onions, cut into halves and cut into $1/4$-inch slices

$2^{1/4}$ cups reduced-sodium beef broth, divided

3 tablespoons Worcestershire sauce

6 hoagie rolls, split

12 slices provolone cheese

1. Season beef with salt and pepper. Heat oil in Dutch oven or large saucepan over medium-high heat. Add beef; cook about 6 minutes per side or until browned. Remove to plate.

2. Add onions and $1/4$ cup broth to Dutch oven; cook 8 minutes or until golden brown, stirring occasionally and scraping up browned bits from bottom of pot. Remove half of onions to small bowl; set aside. Stir in remaining 2 cups broth and Worcestershire sauce; mix well. Return beef to Dutch oven. Reduce heat to low; cover and cook 3 to $3^{1/2}$ hours or until beef is fork-tender.

3. Remove beef to large bowl; let stand until cool enough to handle. Shred beef into bite-size pieces. Add $2/3$ cup cooking liquid; toss to coat. Pour remaining cooking liquid into small bowl for serving.

4. Preheat broiler. Line baking sheet with foil. Place rolls cut side up on prepared baking sheet; broil until lightly browned.

5. Top bottom halves of rolls with cheese, beef and reserved onions. Serve with warm au jus for dipping.

Taco-Topped Potatoes

MAKES 4 SERVINGS

4 Yukon Gold or red potatoes (about 6 ounces each), scrubbed and pierced with fork

8 ounces ground beef

1/2 (1-ounce) package taco seasoning mix

1/2 cup water

1 cup diced tomatoes

1/4 teaspoon salt

2 cups shredded lettuce

1/2 cup (2 ounces) shredded sharp Cheddar cheese

1/4 cup finely chopped green onions

1/2 cup sour cream

1. Microwave potatoes on HIGH 6 to 7 minutes or until fork-tender.

2. Cook beef in large skillet over medium-high heat 6 to 8 minutes or until browned, stirring to break up meat. Drain fat. Add taco seasoning mix and water; cook and stir 1 minute. Remove from heat.

3. Combine tomatoes and salt in medium bowl; mix well.

4. Split potatoes almost in half and fluff with fork. Fill with beef mixture, tomatoes, lettuce, cheese and green onions. Serve with sour cream.

Garlic Pork with Roasted Red Potatoes

MAKES 4 SERVINGS

1 teaspoon salt, divided

1/2 teaspoon paprika

1/2 teaspoon garlic powder

1 pound pork tenderloin

2 tablespoons olive oil, divided

8 unpeeled new red potatoes (about 1 pound), scrubbed and quartered

1 teaspoon dried oregano

1/2 teaspoon black pepper

1. Preheat oven to 425°F. Spray 13×9-inch baking pan with nonstick cooking spray.

2. Combine 1/2 teaspoon salt, paprika and garlic powder in small bowl; sprinkle evenly over pork.

3. Heat 1 tablespoon oil in large skillet over medium-high heat. Add pork; cook about 3 minutes per side or until browned. Place in center of prepared pan.

4. Remove skillet from heat. Add remaining 1 tablespoon oil, potatoes, oregano and remaining 1/2 teaspoon salt; stir to coat potatoes and scrape up browned bits from bottom of skillet. Spoon potato mixture around pork in prepared pan. Sprinkle pork and potatoes with pepper.

5. Bake about 22 minutes or until pork is 145°F. Remove pork to cutting board; tent with foil and let stand 5 minutes before slicing. Serve pork with potatoes.

Chili Spaghetti Casserole

MAKES 6 SERVINGS

8 ounces uncooked spaghetti

1 pound ground beef

1 medium onion, chopped

$1/4$ teaspoon salt

$1/8$ teaspoon black pepper

1 can (about 15 ounces) vegetarian chili with beans

1 can (about 14 ounces) Italian-style stewed tomatoes, undrained

$1^1/2$ cups (6 ounces) shredded sharp Cheddar cheese, divided

$1/2$ cup sour cream

$1^1/2$ teaspoons chili powder

$1/4$ teaspoon garlic powder

1. Preheat oven to 350°F. Spray 13×9-inch baking dish with nonstick cooking spray.

2. Cook spaghetti according to package directions; drain and place in prepared baking dish.

3. Meanwhile, combine beef and onion in large skillet; season with salt and pepper. Cook over medium-high heat 6 to 8 minutes or until browned, stirring to break up meat. Drain fat. Stir in chili, tomatoes, 1 cup cheese, sour cream, chili powder and garlic powder; mix well.

4. Add chili mixture to spaghetti; stir until well blended. Sprinkle with remaining $1/2$ cup cheese. Cover tightly with foil.

5. Bake 30 minutes or until hot and bubbly. Let stand 5 minutes before serving.

Yankee Pot Roast and Vegetables

MAKES 10 TO 12 SERVINGS

1 boneless beef chuck pot roast (2½ pounds)

1 teaspoon salt

½ teaspoon black pepper

3 unpeeled baking potatoes (about 1 pound), cut into quarters

2 carrots, cut into ¾-inch slices

2 stalks celery, cut into ¾-inch slices

1 onion, sliced

1 parsnip, cut into ¾-inch slices

2 bay leaves

1 teaspoon dried rosemary

½ teaspoon dried thyme

½ cup reduced-sodium beef broth

Slow Cooker Directions

1. Trim excess fat from beef. Cut into ¾-inch pieces; sprinkle with salt and pepper.

2. Combine potatoes, carrots, celery, onion, parsnip, bay leaves, rosemary and thyme in slow cooker; top with beef. Pour broth over beef.

3. Cover; cook on LOW 8½ to 9 hours or until beef is fork-tender. Transfer beef and vegetables to serving platter. Remove and discard bay leaves.

Tip: To make gravy, ladle the cooking liquid into a 2-cup measure; let stand 5 minutes. Skim off fat. Heat the cooking liquid to a boil in a small saucepan over medium-high heat. For each cup of liquid, combine 2 tablespoons flour and ¼ cup cold water in a small bowl until smooth; add to the boiling liquid. Cook and stir constantly 1 minute or until thickened.

Pork Schnitzel with Mushroom Gravy

MAKES 6 SERVINGS

6 thin-cut boneless pork sirloin chops or boneless pork loin chops (about 1¼ pounds)*

Salt and black pepper

½ cup plus 1 tablespoon all-purpose flour, divided

2 eggs

1 cup plain dry bread crumbs

2 tablespoons chopped fresh parsley or 1 tablespoon dried parsley flakes

¼ cup vegetable oil

4 tablespoons (½ stick) butter, divided

¼ cup finely chopped onion

1 package (8 ounces) sliced mushrooms

1 cup chicken broth

2 to 3 tablespoons half-and-half

*Pork cutlets can be substituted for the boneless pork chops.

1. Pound pork chops to ⅛-inch thickness with meat mallet or rolling pin. Season with salt and pepper. Place ½ cup flour in shallow dish. Beat eggs in separate shallow dish. Combine bread crumbs and parsley in third shallow dish.

2. Coat pork chops with flour, shaking off excess. Dip into eggs, then into bread crumb mixture, turning to coat.

3. Heat oil and 2 tablespoons butter in large skillet over medium heat. Cook pork chops in two batches about 3 minutes per side or until browned. Remove to plate; tent with foil to keep warm.

4. Melt remaining 2 tablespoons butter in same skillet over medium heat. Add onion; cook and stir 1 minute. Add mushrooms; cook and stir 6 to 7 minutes or until mushrooms are lightly browned and most of moisture has evaporated. Add remaining 1 tablespoon flour; cook and stir 1 minute. Add broth; bring to a boil, stirring constantly. Boil 1 minute. Remove from heat; stir in half-and-half.

5. Spoon gravy over pork chops. Serve immediately.

Beef Fried Rice

MAKES 4 SERVINGS

12 ounces ground beef
6 green onions, chopped
3 large stalks celery, chopped
8 ounces bean sprouts
½ cup sliced mushrooms

½ cup finely chopped red bell pepper
1 teaspoon grated fresh ginger
3 cups cooked rice
2 tablespoons soy sauce
  Salt and black pepper

1. Cook beef in large skillet over medium-high heat 6 to 8 minutes or until browned, stirring to break up meat. Drain fat.

2. Stir in green onions, celery, bean sprouts, mushrooms, bell pepper and ginger; cook over medium-high heat 5 minutes or until vegetables are crisp-tender, stirring frequently.

3. Stir in rice and soy sauce; season with salt and black pepper to taste. Cook until heated through, stirring occasionally.

Beef Fajitas

MAKES 4 SERVINGS

1 teaspoon ground cumin

1 teaspoon dried oregano

12 ounces boneless beef top sirloin steak (about $3/4$ inch thick)

1 tablespoon vegetable oil, divided

2 bell peppers (red, yellow, green or a combination), cut into 1-inch thin strips

$1/2$ cup thinly sliced yellow or red onion

4 cloves garlic, minced

$1/2$ cup spicy salsa

4 (8-inch) flour tortillas, warmed

$1/4$ cup chopped fresh cilantro

1. Rub cumin and oregano over both sides of steak. Heat $1/2$ tablespoon oil in large skillet over medium-high heat. Add steak; cook 3 to 4 minutes per side for medium rare doneness. Remove to cutting board; tent with foil and let rest while cooking vegetables.

2. Add remaining $1/2$ tablespoon oil to same skillet; heat over medium heat. Add bell peppers, onion and garlic; cook and stir 4 to 5 minutes or until vegetables are crisp-tender. Stir in salsa; cook 3 minutes.

3. Cut steak into thin slices; return to skillet. Cook and stir about 1 minute or until heated through. Spoon mixture down center of tortillas; top with cilantro.

MEATLESS MEALS

Vegetable Penne Italiano

MAKES 4 SERVINGS

1 tablespoon olive oil

1 red bell pepper, cut into ½-inch pieces

1 green bell pepper, cut into ½-inch pieces

1 medium sweet onion, halved and thinly sliced

3 cloves garlic, minced

2 tablespoons tomato paste

2 teaspoons salt

1 teaspoon sugar

1 teaspoon Italian seasoning

¼ teaspoon black pepper

1 can (28 ounces) Italian plum tomatoes, undrained, chopped

8 ounces uncooked penne pasta

Grated Parmesan cheese

Chopped fresh basil

1. Heat oil in large skillet over medium-high heat. Add bell peppers, onion and garlic; cook and stir 8 minutes or until vegetables are crisp-tender.

2. Add tomato paste, salt, sugar, Italian seasoning and black pepper; cook and stir 1 minute. Stir in tomatoes with juice. Reduce heat to medium-low; cook 15 minutes or until vegetables are tender and sauce is thickened.

3. Meanwhile, cook pasta in large saucepan of salted boiling water according to package directions until al dente. Drain and return to saucepan. Pour sauce over pasta; stir gently to coat. Top with cheese and basil.

Spanakopita

MAKES 4 SERVINGS

1 tablespoon olive oil

1 large onion, cut into quarters and thinly sliced

2 cloves garlic, minced

1 package (10 ounces) frozen chopped spinach, thawed and squeezed dry

½ cup (2 ounces) crumbled feta cheese

5 sheets phyllo dough, thawed*

¼ cup (½ stick) butter, melted

2 eggs

¼ teaspoon salt

¼ teaspoon ground nutmeg

¼ teaspoon black pepper

*Thaw entire package of phyllo dough overnight in refrigerator.

1. Preheat oven to 375°F. Spray 8-inch square baking pan with nonstick cooking spray.

2. Heat oil in large skillet over medium heat. Add onion; cook and stir 7 to 8 minutes or until soft. Add garlic; cook and stir 30 seconds. Add spinach and cheese; cook and stir until spinach is heated through. Remove from heat; set aside to cool.

3. Place one sheet phyllo dough on counter with long side toward you. (Cover remaining sheets with damp towel until needed to prevent drying out.) Brush right half of phyllo lightly with melted butter; fold left half over buttered half. Place sheet in prepared pan. (Two edges will hang over sides of pan.) Brush top of sheet lightly with butter. Brush and fold two more sheets of phyllo the same way. Arrange phyllo sheets in pan at 90-degree angles so edges will hang over all four sides of pan. Brush each sheet lightly with butter after placing in pan.

4. Beat eggs, salt, nutmeg and pepper in small bowl until blended. Add to spinach mixture; stir until blended. Spread filling over phyllo in pan. Brush and fold one sheet phyllo as above; place over filling, tucking ends under filling. Bring all overhanging edges of phyllo over top sheet; brush lightly with butter. Brush and fold remaining phyllo sheet as above; place over top sheet, tucking ends under. Brush with butter.

5. Bake about 25 minutes or until top is lightly browned. Cool 10 to 15 minutes before serving.

Macaroni and Cheese

MAKES 8 SERVINGS

1 package (16 ounces) uncooked elbow macaroni

¼ cup (½ stick) butter

¼ cup all-purpose flour

½ teaspoon salt

½ teaspoon dry mustard

¼ teaspoon black pepper

3 cups milk

4 cups (16 ounces) shredded sharp Cheddar cheese

Paprika

¼ cup shredded Parmesan cheese (optional)

Fresh thyme leaves (optional)

1. Preheat oven to 350°F. Spray 13×9-inch baking dish or 3-quart casserole with nonstick cooking spray.

2. Cook pasta in large saucepan according to package directions; drain and return to saucepan.

3. Melt butter in medium saucepan over medium-low heat. Whisk in flour, salt, mustard and pepper; cook and stir 1 minute. Whisk in milk. Bring to a boil over medium heat, stirring frequently. Reduce heat to low; cook 2 minutes. Remove from heat. Add Cheddar; stir until melted. Pour cheese mixture over pasta; stir gently to coat. Transfer to prepared baking dish; sprinkle with paprika.

4. Bake, uncovered, 20 to 25 minutes or until hot and bubbly. Sprinkle with Parmesan and thyme, if desired.

Mexican Tortilla Stack-Ups

MAKES 6 SERVINGS

1 tablespoon vegetable oil

½ cup chopped onion

1 can (about 15 ounces) black beans, rinsed and drained

1 can (about 14 ounces) Mexican- or Italian-seasoned diced tomatoes

1 cup frozen corn

1 package (1 ounce) taco seasoning mix

6 (6-inch) corn tortillas

2 cups (8 ounces) shredded Mexican cheese blend

1 cup water

Sliced black olives (optional)

1. Preheat oven to 350°F. Spray 13×9-inch baking dish with nonstick cooking spray.

2. Heat oil in large skillet over medium-high heat. Add onion; cook and stir 3 minutes or until tender. Add beans, tomatoes, corn and taco seasoning mix; bring to a boil over high heat. Reduce heat to low; simmer 5 minutes.

3. Place two tortillas side by side in prepared baking dish. Top each tortilla with about ½ cup bean mixture; sprinkle with one third of cheese. Repeat layers twice. Pour water around edges of tortillas.

4. Cover with foil and bake 30 to 35 minutes or until heated through. Cut into wedges; sprinkle with olives, if desired.

Sesame Noodles

MAKES 6 TO 8 SERVINGS

1 package (16 ounces) uncooked spaghetti

6 tablespoons soy sauce

5 tablespoons toasted sesame oil

3 tablespoons sugar

3 tablespoons rice vinegar

2 tablespoons vegetable oil

3 cloves garlic, minced

1 teaspoon grated fresh ginger

½ teaspoon sriracha

2 green onions, sliced

1 red bell pepper

1 cucumber

1 carrot

Sesame seeds (optional)

1. Cook spaghetti in large saucepan of boiling salted water according to package directions until al dente. Drain spaghetti, reserving 1 tablespoon cooking water.

2. Whisk soy sauce, sesame oil, sugar, vinegar, vegetable oil, garlic, ginger, sriracha and reserved cooking water in large bowl until well blended. Stir in spaghetti and green onions. Let stand at least 30 minutes until spaghetti has cooled to room temperature and most of sauce is absorbed, stirring occasionally.

3. Meanwhile, cut bell pepper into thin strips. Peel cucumber and carrot and shred with julienne peeler into long strands or cut into thin strips. Stir vegetables into spaghetii. Serve at room temperature or refrigerate until ready to serve. Top with sesame seeds, if desired.

Portobello Grilled Cheese

MAKES 4 SERVINGS

2 portobello mushroom caps, thinly sliced

1 small red onion, thinly sliced

1 cup grape tomatoes

2 tablespoons olive oil

2 teaspoons balsamic vinegar

¼ teaspoon salt

¼ teaspoon dried thyme

¼ teaspoon black pepper

4 tablespoons butter, softened, divided

8 slices sourdough bread

4 slices provolone cheese

4 teaspoons Dijon mustard

4 slices Monterey Jack cheese

1. Preheat broiler. Combine mushroom, onion and tomatoes in medium baking pan. Drizzle with oil and vinegar; sprinkle with salt, thyme and pepper and toss to coat. Spread vegetables in single layer in pan.

2. Broil 6 minutes or until vegetables are softened and browned, stirring once.

3. Heat large skillet over medium heat. Spread half of butter over one side of each bread slice. Place bread buttered side down in skillet; cook 2 minutes or until toasted. Transfer bread to cutting board, toasted sides up.

4. Place provolone cheese on two bread slices; spread mustard over cheese. Top with vegetables, Monterey Jack cheese and remaining bread slices, toasted sides down. Spread remaining half of butter on outside of sandwiches. Cook in same skillet over medium heat 5 minutes or until bread is toasted and cheese is melted, turning once.

Bell Pepper and Ricotta Calzones

MAKES 6 SERVINGS

- 1 tablespoon olive oil
- 1 medium red bell pepper, chopped
- 1 medium green bell pepper, chopped
- 1 small onion, chopped
- 1/2 teaspoon salt
- 1/2 teaspoon Italian seasoning
- 1/8 teaspoon black pepper
- 1 clove garlic, minced
- 1 1/4 cups marinara sauce, divided
- 1/4 cup ricotta cheese
- 1/4 cup shredded mozzarella cheese
- 1 package (about 14 ounces) refrigerated pizza dough

1. Preheat oven to 375°F. Line baking sheet with parchment paper or spray with nonstick cooking spray.

2. Heat oil in large skillet over medium heat. Add bell peppers, onion, salt, Italian seasoning and black pepper; cook about 8 minutes or until vegetables are tender, stirring occasionally. Add garlic; cook and stir 1 minute. Stir in 1/2 cup marinara sauce; cook about 2 minutes or until slightly thickened. Remove from heat; set aside to cool slightly.

3. Combine ricotta and mozzarella in small bowl; mix well. Unroll dough on work surface; cut into six 4-inch squares. Pat each square into 5-inch square. Spoon 1/3 cup vegetable mixture into center of each square; sprinkle with heaping tablespoon cheese mixture. Fold dough over filling to form triangle; pinch and fold edges together to seal. Transfer calzones to prepared baking sheet.

4. Bake 15 to 18 minutes or until calzones are lightly browned. Cool 5 minutes. Serve with remaining marinara sauce.

Vegetable Enchiladas

MAKES 6 SERVINGS

1 tablespoon vegetable oil

2 large poblano peppers or green bell peppers, cut into 2-inch strips

1 large zucchini, cut into 2-inch strips

1 large red onion, sliced

1 cup sliced mushrooms

1 teaspoon ground cumin

1 pound fresh tomatillos (about 8 large), peeled

1 small jalapeño pepper, minced

1 clove garlic

1/2 teaspoon salt

1 cup loosely packed fresh cilantro

12 corn tortillas, warmed

2 cups (8 ounces) shredded Mexican cheese blend, divided

1. Preheat oven to 400°F. Heat oil in large skillet over medium heat. Add poblano peppers, zucchini, onion, mushrooms and cumin; cook 8 to 10 minutes or until vegetables are crisp-tender, stirring occasionally.

2. Meanwhile, place tomatillos in large microwavable bowl. Cover with vented plastic wrap; microwave on HIGH 6 to 7 minutes or until very tender.

3. Combine tomatillos with juice, jalapeño, garlic and salt in food processor or blender; process until smooth. Add 1 cup cilantro; pulse until combined and cilantro is coarsely chopped.

4. Divide vegetables evenly among tortillas. Spoon heaping tablespoon of cheese in center of each tortilla; roll up to enclose filling. Place in 13×9-inch baking dish. Pour sauce evenly over enchiladas; sprinkle with remaining 1 cup cheese.

5. Cover and bake 18 to 20 minutes or until cheese is melted and enchiladas are heated through. Serve immediately.

Baked Ravioli with Pumpkin Sauce

MAKES 4 SERVINGS

1 package (9 ounces) refrigerated cheese ravioli

1 tablespoon butter

1 shallot, finely chopped

1 cup whipping cream

1 cup canned pumpkin

$\frac{1}{2}$ cup grated Asiago cheese, divided

$\frac{1}{2}$ teaspoon salt

$\frac{1}{4}$ teaspoon ground nutmeg

$\frac{1}{8}$ teaspoon black pepper

$\frac{1}{2}$ cup coarse plain dry bread crumbs or small croutons

1. Preheat oven to 350°F. Spray 2-quart baking dish with nonstick cooking spray.

2. Cook ravioli according to package directions. Drain well; cover to keep warm.

3. Meanwhile, melt butter in medium saucepan over medium heat. Add shallot; cook and stir 3 minutes or until tender. Reduce heat to low. Add cream, pumpkin, $\frac{1}{4}$ cup cheese, salt, nutmeg and pepper; cook and stir 2 minutes or until cheese melts. Add ravioli; stir gently to coat.

4. Spoon ravioli mixture into prepared baking dish. Combine remaining $\frac{1}{4}$ cup cheese and bread crumbs in small bowl; sprinkle over ravioli.

5. Bake 15 minutes or until heated through and topping is lightly browned.

Sweet Potato and Black Bean Chipotle Chili

MAKES 8 TO 10 SERVINGS

1 tablespoon vegetable oil
2 large onions, diced
1 tablespoon minced garlic
2 tablespoons tomato paste
3 tablespoons chili powder
1 tablespoon chipotle chili powder
1 teaspoon ground cumin
2 teaspoons kosher salt
1 cup water

1 large sweet potato, peeled and cut into $\frac{1}{2}$-inch pieces (about 2 pounds)
2 cans (28 ounces each) black beans, rinsed and drained
2 cans (28 ounces each) crushed tomatoes
Optional toppings: sour cream, sliced green onions, shredded cheddar cheese and/or tortilla chips

Slow Cooker Directions

1. Heat oil in large skillet over medium-high heat. Add onions; cook 8 minutes or until softened and lightly browned.

2. Add garlic, tomato paste, chili powder, chipotle chili powder, cumin and salt; cook and stir 1 minute. Stir in water, scraping up browned bits from bottom of skillet. Transfer to slow cooker; stir in sweet potato, beans and tomatoes.

3. Cover; cook on LOW 8 hours or on HIGH 4 hours. Serve with desired toppings.

Spinach Stuffed Manicotti

MAKES 4 SERVINGS

8 uncooked manicotti shells
1 tablespoon olive oil
1 teaspoon minced garlic
1 teaspoon dried rosemary
1 teaspoon dried sage
1 teaspoon dried oregano
1 teaspoon dried thyme
1½ cups chopped fresh tomatoes

¾ teaspoon salt, divided
1 package (10 ounces) frozen spinach, thawed and squeezed dry
½ cup ricotta cheese
½ cup fresh bread crumbs
1 egg, lightly beaten

1. Cook manicotti according to package directions, drain and rinse under cold water until cool enough to handle. Preheat oven to 350°F.

2. Heat oil in medium saucepan over medium heat. Add garlic, rosemary, sage, oregano and thyme; cook and stir 1 minute. Stir in tomatoes and ½ teaspoon salt. Reduce heat to low; simmer 10 minutes, stirring occasionally.

3. Combine spinach, cheese, bread crumbs, egg and remaining ¼ teaspoon salt in medium bowl; mix well. Fill manicotti with spinach mixture.

4. Pour one third of tomato sauce into 13×9-inch baking dish. Place filled manicotti in single layer in sauce; pour remaining tomato sauce over manicotti.

5. Cover with foil; bake 30 minutes or until hot and bubbly.

Red, White and Black Bean Casserole

MAKES 6 SERVINGS

2 tablespoons olive oil

1 yellow or green bell pepper, cut into 1/2-inch strips

1/2 cup sliced green onions

1 jar (14 to 16 ounces) chunky salsa

1 can (4 ounces) diced green chiles, drained

2 tablespoons chopped fresh cilantro

1 package (1 ounce) taco seasoning mix

1/2 teaspoon salt

2 cups cooked rice

1 can (about 15 ounces) cannellini beans, rinsed and drained

1 can (about 15 ounces) red kidney beans, rinsed and drained

1 can (about 15 ounces) black beans, rinsed and drained

1 cup (4 ounces) shredded Cheddar cheese, divided

Flour tortillas, warmed (optional)

1. Preheat oven to 350°F. Spray 13×9-inch baking dish with nonstick cooking spray.

2. Heat oil in large saucepan over medium-high heat. Add bell pepper and green onions; cook and stir 5 minutes. Add salsa, chiles, cilantro, taco seasoning mix and salt; cook 5 minutes, stirring occasionally. Stir in rice and beans. Remove from heat; stir in 1/2 cup cheese. Spoon mixture into prepared baking dish; sprinkle with remaining 1/2 cup cheese.

3. Cover and bake 30 to 40 minutes or until heated through. Serve with warm tortillas, if desired.

VEGETABLES & SIDES

Crispy Smashed Potatoes

MAKES ABOUT 6 SERVINGS

1 tablespoon plus $\frac{1}{2}$ teaspoon salt, divided

3 pounds unpeeled small red potatoes (2 inches or smaller)

4 tablespoons olive oil, divided

$\frac{1}{4}$ teaspoon black pepper

1. Fill large saucepan three-fourths full of water; add 1 tablespoon salt. Bring to a boil over high heat. Add potatoes; boil about 20 minutes or until potatoes are tender when pierced with tip of sharp knife. Drain potatoes; set aside until cool enough to handle.

2. Preheat oven to 450°F. Brush baking sheet with 2 tablespoons oil. Working with one potato at a time, smash with hand or bottom of measuring cup to about $\frac{1}{2}$-inch thickness. Arrange smashed potatoes in single layer on prepared baking sheet. Brush potatoes with remaining 2 tablespoons oil; sprinkle with remaining $\frac{1}{2}$ teaspoon salt and pepper.

3. Bake 30 to 40 minutes or until bottoms of potatoes are golden brown. Turn potatoes; bake 10 minutes or until crisp and browned on bottoms.

Cheesy Spinach Casserole

MAKES 6 SERVINGS

1 pound baby spinach
4 slices bacon, chopped
1 small onion, chopped
1 cup sliced mushrooms
1/4 cup chopped red bell pepper
3 cloves garlic, minced
1 1/2 teaspoons minced canned chipotle peppers in adobo sauce

1 teaspoon seasoned salt
8 ounces pasteurized process cheese product, cut into pieces
1/2 (8-ounce) package cream cheese, cut into pieces
1 cup thawed frozen corn
1/2 cup (2 ounces) shredded Monterey Jack and Cheddar cheese blend

1. Preheat oven to 350°F. Spray 1-quart baking dish with nonstick cooking spray.

2. Heat large saucepan of water to a boil over high heat. Add spinach; cook 1 minute. Drain and transfer to bowl of ice water to stop cooking. Drain and squeeze spinach dry; set aside. Wipe out saucepan with paper towel.

3. Cook bacon in same saucepan over medium-high heat until almost crisp, stirring frequently. Drain off all but 1 tablespoon drippings. Add onion to saucepan; cook and stir 3 minutes or until softened. Add mushrooms and bell pepper; cook and stir 5 minutes or until vegetables are tender. Add garlic, chipotle peppers and seasoned salt; cook and stir 1 minute.

4. Add cheese product and cream cheese to saucepan; cook over medium heat until melted, stirring frequently. Add spinach and corn; cook and stir 3 minutes. Transfer to prepared baking dish; sprinkle with shredded cheese.

5. Bake 20 to 25 minutes or until cheese is melted and casserole is bubbly. If desired, broil 1 to 2 minutes to brown top of casserole.

— Spanish Rice —

MAKES 6 TO 8 SERVINGS

1 tablespoon olive oil
1 small onion, chopped
2 cloves garlic, minced
2 cups uncooked brown rice, rinsed well and drained

1 can (about 14 ounces) diced tomatoes with green chiles
3½ cups water or chicken broth
1½ teaspoons salt

1. Heat oil in medium saucepan over medium-high heat. Add onion and garlic; cook and stir 2 minutes. Add rice; cook and stir 2 minutes.

2. Stir in tomatoes, water and salt; bring to a boil. Reduce heat to low; cover and simmer 35 to 40 minutes or until rice is tender and water is absorbed. Fluff rice with fork.

Orange Glazed Carrots

MAKES 6 SERVINGS

1 package (32 ounces) baby carrots
1 tablespoon packed brown sugar
1 tablespoon orange juice

1 tablespoon melted butter
¼ teaspoon salt
¼ teaspoon ground cinnamon
⅛ teaspoon ground nutmeg

1. Bring 1 inch of lightly salted water to a boil in medium saucepan over high heat. Add carrots; return to a boil. Reduce heat to low; cover and simmer 10 to 12 minutes or until crisp-tender. Drain well; return carrots to saucepan.

2. Stir in brown sugar, orange juice, butter, salt, cinnamon and nutmeg; cook over medium heat 3 minutes or until carrots are glazed, stirring occasionally.

SPANISH RICE

Super Simple Bubble Loaf

MAKES 12 SERVINGS

2 packages (12 ounces each) refrigerated buttermilk biscuits (10 biscuits per package)

2 tablespoons butter, melted

1½ cups (6 ounces) shredded Italian cheese blend

1. Preheat oven to 350°F. Spray 9×5-inch loaf pan with nonstick cooking spray.

2. Separate biscuits; cut each biscuit into four pieces with scissors. Layer half of biscuit pieces in prepared pan. Drizzle with 1 tablespoon butter; sprinkle with 1 cup cheese. Top with remaining biscuit pieces, 1 tablespoon butter and ½ cup cheese.

3. Bake 25 minutes or until golden brown. Serve warm.

Tip: It's easy to change up the flavors in this simple bread. Try Mexican cheese blend instead of Italian, and add taco seasoning mix and/or hot pepper sauce to the melted butter before drizzling it over the dough. Or, sprinkle ¼ cup chopped ham, salami or crumbled crisp-cooked bacon between the layers of dough.

Broccoli and Cheese

MAKES 4 TO 6 SERVINGS

2 medium crowns broccoli (1½ pounds), cut into florets (about 6½ cups)

2 tablespoons butter

2 tablespoons all-purpose flour

1½ cups milk

½ teaspoon salt

⅛ teaspoon ground nutmeg

⅛ teaspoon ground red pepper

1 cup (4 ounces) shredded Cheddar cheese

½ cup (2 ounces) shredded Monterey Jack cheese

¼ cup shredded Parmesan cheese Paprika (optional)

1. Bring large saucepan of water to a boil over medium-high heat. Add broccoli; cook 7 minutes or until tender.

2. Meanwhile, melt butter in medium saucepan over medium-high heat. Add flour; whisk until smooth. Gradually whisk in milk until well blended. Cook 2 minutes or until thickened, whisking frequently. Stir in salt, nutmeg and red pepper. Reduce heat to low; whisk in cheeses in three additions, whisking well after first two additions and stirring just until blended after last addition.

3. Drain broccoli; place on serving plates. Top with cheese sauce; garnish with paprika. Serve immediately.

Corn Soufflé

MAKES 6 SERVINGS

3 tablespoons all-purpose flour
1 tablespoon sugar
½ teaspoon black pepper
3 eggs
2 cups frozen whole kernel corn, thawed and drained
1 can (about 15 ounces) cream-style corn

1 cup (4 ounces) shredded Mexican cheese blend or Monterey Jack cheese
⅓ cup milk
1 jar (2 ounces) chopped pimientos, drained

1. Preheat oven to 350°F. Spray 8-inch round baking dish with nonstick cooking spray.

2. Combine flour, sugar and pepper in large bowl; mix well. Add eggs; beat with electric mixer at high speed until smooth. Stir in corn kernels, cream-style corn, cheese, milk and pimientos until well blended. Pour into prepared baking dish.

3. Bake 55 minutes or until set. Let stand 15 minutes before serving.

New England Baked Beans

MAKES 4 TO 6 SERVINGS

4 slices bacon, chopped

3 cans (about 15 ounces each) Great Northern beans, rinsed and drained

3/4 cup water

1 onion, chopped

1/3 cup canned diced tomatoes, well drained

3 tablespoons packed brown sugar

3 tablespoons maple syrup

3 tablespoons molasses

2 cloves garlic, minced

1/2 teaspoon salt

1/2 teaspoon dry mustard

1/8 teaspoon black pepper

1 bay leaf

Slow Cooker Directions

1. Cook bacon in large skillet over medium-high heat until almost chewy but not crisp. Drain on paper towel-lined plate.

2. Combine bacon, beans, water, onion, tomatoes, brown sugar, maple syrup, molasses, garlic, salt, mustard, pepper and bay leaf in slow cooker; mix well.

3. Cover; cook on LOW 6 to 8 hours or until thickened. Remove and discard bay leaf.

Cheesy Garlic Bread

MAKES 8 TO 10 SERVINGS

1 loaf (about 16 ounces) Italian bread

½ cup (1 stick) butter, softened

8 cloves garlic, very thinly sliced

¼ cup grated Parmesan cheese

2 cups (8 ounces) shredded mozzarella cheese

1. Preheat oven to 425°F. Line large baking sheet with foil.

2. Cut bread in half horizontally. Spread cut sides of bread evenly with butter; top with sliced garlic. Sprinkle with Parmesan, then mozzarella. Place on prepared baking sheet.

3. Bake 12 minutes or until cheeses are melted and golden brown in spots. Cut bread crosswise into slices. Serve warm.

Chunky Applesauce

MAKES ABOUT 5½ CUPS

10 tart apples (about 3 pounds), peeled and chopped

¾ cup packed brown sugar

½ cup apple juice or apple cider

1½ teaspoons ground cinnamon

⅛ teaspoon salt

⅛ teaspoon ground nutmeg

1. Combine apples, brown sugar, apple juice, cinnamon, salt and nutmeg in large saucepan; cover and cook over medium-low heat 40 to 45 minutes or until apples are tender, stirring occasionally.

2. Remove from heat; cool completely. Store in airtight container in refrigerator up to 1 month.

CHEESY GARLIC BREAD

Creamy Parmesan Spinach

MAKES 4 TO 6 SERVINGS

2 tablespoons butter, divided

1 cup finely chopped yellow onion

2 packages (9 ounces each) fresh spinach, divided

3 ounces cream cheese, cut into pieces

1/2 teaspoon garlic powder

1/4 teaspoon salt

1/4 teaspoon black pepper

1/4 teaspoon ground nutmeg

1/4 cup grated Parmesan or Monterey Jack cheese, divided

1. Melt 1 tablespoon butter in large skillet over medium-high heat. Add onion; cook and stir 4 minutes or until translucent.

2. Add one package of spinach; cook and stir 2 minutes or just until wilted. Transfer spinach mixture to medium bowl. Repeat with remaining 1 tablespoon butter and spinach.

3. Return reserved spinach to skillet. Add cream cheese, garlic powder, salt, pepper and nutmeg; cook and stir until cream cheese has completely melted.

4. Stir in 2 tablespoons Parmesan. Sprinkle with remaining 2 tablespoons Parmesan just before serving.

Tip: For a thinner consistency, add 2 to 3 tablespoons milk before adding the Parmesan cheese.

Sweet Potato and Apple Casserole

MAKES 9 SERVINGS

1 cup all-purpose flour

3/4 cup (1 1/2 sticks) butter, melted, divided

1/2 cup packed brown sugar

1/2 teaspoon salt

1/2 teaspoon ground cinnamon

1/4 teaspoon ground nutmeg or mace

1/4 teaspoon ground cardamom

2 pounds sweet potatoes, peeled, halved lengthwise and thinly sliced

2 Granny Smith apples, peeled, cored, halved lengthwise and thinly sliced

1. Preheat oven to 375°F. Spray 2-quart baking dish with nonstick cooking spray.

2. Combine flour, 1/2 cup butter, brown sugar, 1/2 teaspoon salt, cinnamon, nutmeg and cardamom in medium bowl; mix well.

3. Arrange sweet potatoes and apples in prepared baking dish. Drizzle with remaining 1/4 cup butter; season lightly with additional salt. Crumble flour mixture over sweet potatoes and apples.

4. Bake 35 to 40 minutes or until topping is browned and sweet potatoes and apples are tender.

Jalapeño Cheddar Corn Bread

MAKES 8 SERVINGS

1 cup yellow cornmeal
³/₄ cup all-purpose flour
¹/₃ cup sugar
2 teaspoons baking powder
1 teaspoon salt
1 cup buttermilk or whole milk

2 eggs
3 tablespoons butter, melted
1 cup (4 ounces) shredded Cheddar cheese
2 jalapeño peppers, seeded and minced (about ¹/₃ cup)

1. Preheat oven to 400°F. Spray 8-inch round baking pan with nonstick cooking spray.

2. Combine cornmeal, flour, sugar, baking powder and salt in large bowl; mix well. Whisk buttermilk, eggs and butter in medium bowl until blended. Add to cornmeal mixture; stir just until blended. Stir in cheese and jalapeños until blended. Spread batter evenly in prepared pan.

3. Bake 18 to 20 minutes or until top is golden brown and toothpick inserted into center comes out clean. Cool in pan on wire rack 10 minutes; remove to serving plate. Cut into wedges.

DESSERTS

Blueberry Crumb Cake

MAKES 12 TO 15 SERVINGS

Crumb Topping
(recipe follows)
2 cups all-purpose flour
2/3 cup sugar
1 tablespoon baking powder
1 teaspoon salt
1/2 teaspoon baking soda

1 cup milk
1/2 cup (1 stick) butter, melted
2 eggs
2 tablespoons lemon juice
2 cups fresh or thawed frozen
   blueberries

1. Preheat oven to 375°F. Spray 13×9-inch baking pan with nonstick cooking spray. Prepare Crumb Topping.

2. Sift flour, sugar, baking powder, salt and baking soda into large bowl. Whisk milk, butter, eggs and lemon juice in medium bowl until well blended. Add to flour mixture; stir until blended. Pour batter into prepared pan.

3. Sprinkle blueberries evenly over batter; sprinkle with Crumb Topping.

4. Bake 40 to 45 minutes or until toothpick inserted into center comes out clean. Serve warm.

Crumb Topping: Combine 1 cup chopped walnuts or pecans, 2/3 cup sugar, 1/2 cup all-purpose flour, 1/4 cup (1/2 stick) softened butter and 1/2 teaspoon ground cinnamon in large bowl until mixture forms coarse crumbs.

Lemon Cheesecake

MAKES 12 SERVINGS

9 graham crackers, crushed into crumbs

$1/3$ cup ground blanched almonds

6 tablespoons ($3/4$ stick) butter, melted

$3/4$ cup plus 2 tablespoons sugar, divided

3 packages (8 ounces each) cream cheese, softened

1 container (15 ounces) ricotta cheese

4 eggs, beaten

2 tablespoons finely grated lemon peel

1 teaspoon lemon extract

1 teaspoon vanilla

1. Preheat oven to 375°F.

2. Combine graham cracker crumbs, almonds, butter and 2 tablespoons sugar in medium bowl; mix well. Press evenly onto bottom and $1/2$ inch up side of 9-inch springform pan. Bake 5 minutes. Remove to wire rack to cool. *Reduce oven temperature to 325°F.*

3. Beat cream cheese, ricotta, eggs, remaining $3/4$ cup sugar, lemon peel, lemon extract and vanilla in large bowl with electric mixer at low speed until blended. Beat at high speed 4 to 5 minutes until smooth and creamy. Pour into crust.

4. Bake 1 hour and 10 minutes or until just set in center. *Do not overbake.* Remove to wire rack to cool to room temperature. Cover and refrigerate 4 hours or overnight.

Double Chocolate Pecan Brownies

MAKES 16 BROWNIES

1 cup plus 2 tablespoons all-purpose flour

$^3/_4$ cup unsweetened cocoa powder

$^1/_2$ teaspoon baking powder

$^1/_4$ teaspoon salt

$1^1/_4$ cups sugar

$^1/_2$ cup (1 stick) butter, softened

2 eggs

1 teaspoon vanilla

$^1/_2$ cup semisweet chocolate chips

$^1/_2$ cup chopped pecans

1. Preheat oven to 350°F. Line 8-inch square baking pan with foil, extending foil over two sides of pan. Spray foil with nonstick cooking spray.

2. Combine flour, cocoa, baking powder and salt in medium bowl; mix well.

3. Beat sugar and butter in large bowl with electric mixer at medium speed 2 to 3 minutes or until creamy. Add eggs, one at a time, beating well after each addition. Beat in vanilla. Gradually add flour mixture at low speed, beating just until blended. Spread batter in prepared pan (batter will be very thick). Sprinkle with chocolate chips and pecans.

4. Bake about 30 minutes or until toothpick inserted into center comes out almost clean. Cool in pan 5 minutes; use foil to remove brownies to wire rack to cool completely. Cut into bars.

Apple Snack Cake

MAKES 12 TO 15 SERVINGS

1¼ cups granulated sugar, divided
1 cup (2 sticks) butter, softened
¾ cup packed brown sugar
2 eggs
1 teaspoon vanilla
1 cup buttermilk
2½ cups all-purpose flour
2 teaspoons ground cinnamon, divided

1 teaspoon baking powder
1 teaspoon baking soda
1 teaspoon salt
¼ teaspoon ground nutmeg
3 cups chopped peeled apples
1 cup chopped nuts

1. Preheat oven to 350°F. Spray 13×9-inch baking pan with nonstick cooking spray.

2. Beat ¾ cup granulated sugar, butter, brown sugar, eggs and vanilla in large bowl with electric mixer at medium speed about 3 minutes or until creamy. Add buttermilk; beat until blended.

3. Combine flour, 1 teaspoon cinnamon, baking powder, baking soda, salt and nutmeg in medium bowl; mix well. Add to sugar mixture; beat until blended. Stir in apples. Pour batter into prepared pan.

4. Combine remaining ½ cup granulated sugar, 1 teaspoon cinnamon and nuts in small bowl; mix well. Sprinkle over batter.

5. Bake 35 to 40 minutes or until toothpick inserted into center comes out clean. Cool completely in pan on wire rack.

Banana Cream Pie

MAKES 8 SERVINGS

1 refrigerated pie crust (half of 14-ounce package), at room temperature

$^2/_3$ cup sugar

$^1/_4$ cup cornstarch

$^1/_4$ teaspoon salt

$2^1/_2$ cups milk

4 egg yolks, beaten

2 tablespoons butter, softened

2 teaspoons vanilla

2 medium bananas

1 teaspoon lemon juice

Whipped cream and toasted sliced almonds (optional)

1. Preheat oven to 400°F. Line 9-inch pie plate with crust; flute edge. Prick bottom and side all over with fork. Bake 10 minutes or until crust is golden brown. Cool completely on wire rack.

2. Combine sugar, cornstarch and salt in medium saucepan; whisk in milk until well blended. Cook over medium heat about 12 minutes or until mixture boils and thickens, stirring constantly. Boil 2 minutes, stirring constantly. Remove from heat.

3. Gradually whisk $^1/_2$ hot cup milk mixture into egg yolks in small bowl. Gradually whisk mixture back into milk mixture in saucepan. Cook over medium heat about 5 minutes, whisking constantly. Remove from heat; whisk in butter and vanilla. Cool 20 minutes, stirring occasionally. Strain through fine-mesh strainer into medium bowl. Press plastic wrap onto surface of pudding; cool about 30 minutes or until lukewarm.

4. Cut bananas into $^1/_4$-inch slices; toss with lemon juice in medium bowl. Spread half of pudding in cooled crust; arrange bananas over pudding. (Reserve several slices for garnish, if desired.) Spread remaining pudding over bananas. Refrigerate 4 hours or overnight. Garnish with whipped cream, almonds and reserved banana slices.

Chocolate Eclair Cake

MAKES 12 TO 18 SERVINGS

3¼ cups plus 6 tablespoons whole milk, divided

2 packages (3.4 ounces each) vanilla instant pudding and pie filling mix

1 container (8 ounces) frozen whipped topping, thawed

1⅓ boxes (about 14 ounces each) graham crackers (35 whole graham cracker rectangles)

6 tablespoons (¾ stick) butter

⅓ cup unsweetened dark or regular cocoa powder

Pinch salt

1 teaspoon vanilla

2 cups powdered sugar, sifted

1. Whisk 3¼ cups milk and vanilla pudding mixes in large bowl about 2 minutes. Fold in whipped topping until well blended.

2. Cover bottom of 13×9-inch pan with single layer of graham crackers, cutting to fit as needed. Pour one third of pudding mixture (about 2½ cups) over graham crackers; smooth top with spatula. Repeat layers twice. Top with remaining graham crackers, arranging them bumpy side down over pudding mixture.

3. Combine remaining 6 tablespoons milk and butter in large microwavable bowl; microwave on HIGH 30 seconds. Stir; microwave 30 seconds or until butter is melted. Add cocoa and salt; whisk until blended. Stir in vanilla. Add powdered sugar; whisk until well blended and smooth.

4. Pour chocolate icing over graham crackers, spreading in even layer that covers top completely. Refrigerate 8 hours or overnight.

Snickerdoodles

MAKES ABOUT 3 DOZEN COOKIES

$^3/_4$ cup plus 2 tablespoons sugar, divided

2 teaspoons ground cinnamon, divided

$1^1/_3$ cups all-purpose flour

1 teaspoon cream of tartar

$^1/_2$ teaspoon baking soda

$^1/_2$ teaspoon salt

$^1/_2$ cup (1 stick) butter, softened

1 egg

1. Preheat oven to 375°F. Line cookie sheets with parchment paper.

2. Combine 2 tablespoons sugar and 1 teaspoon cinnamon in small bowl; mix well. Combine flour, remaining 1 teaspoon cinnamon, cream of tartar, baking soda and salt in medium bowl; mix well.

3. Beat remaining $^3/_4$ cup sugar and butter in large bowl with electric mixer at medium speed about 3 minutes or until creamy. Beat in egg until well blended. Gradually add flour mixture, beating at low speed until stiff dough forms. Roll dough into 1-inch balls; roll in cinnamon-sugar mixture to coat. Place 2 inches apart on prepared cookie sheets.

4. Bake 10 minutes or just until cookies are set. Remove to wire racks to cool completely.

Carrot Cake

MAKES 12 TO 15 SERVINGS

2 cups all-purpose flour

2 teaspoons baking soda

2 teaspoons ground cinnamon, plus additional for garnish

1 teaspoon salt

2 cups granulated sugar

1 cup vegetable oil

4 eggs

1 teaspoon vanilla

3 cups finely grated carrots (about 5 medium)

1 cup shredded coconut

1 can (8 ounces) crushed pineapple

1 cup chopped walnuts

Cream Cheese Frosting (recipe follows)

1. Preheat oven to 350°F. Spray 13×9-inch baking pan with nonstick cooking spray.

2. Combine flour, baking soda, 2 teaspoons cinnamon and salt in medium bowl; mix well. Beat granulated sugar and oil in large bowl until well blended. Add eggs, one at a time; beat until well blended. Beat in vanilla. Add flour mixture; stir until blended. Add carrots, coconut, pineapple and walnuts; stir just until blended. Pour batter into prepared pan.

3. Bake 45 to 50 minutes or until toothpick inserted into center comes out clean. Cool completely in pan on wire rack.

4. Prepare frosting; spread over cake. Sprinkle with additional cinnamon, if desired.

Cream Cheese Frosting: Beat 1 package (8 ounces) softened cream cheese, 1/2 cup (1 stick) softened butter and pinch of salt in large bowl with electric mixer at medium speed 3 minutes or until light and creamy. Add 1 1/2 cups powdered sugar, 1 tablespoon milk and 1 teaspoon vanilla; beat at low speed until blended. Beat at medium speed 2 minutes or until frosting is smooth. Add additional milk for softer frosting, if desired.

Extra Chunky Peanut Butter Cookies

MAKES ABOUT 4 DOZEN COOKIES

2 cups all-purpose flour
1 teaspoon baking soda
1/2 teaspoon salt
1 cup chunky peanut butter
3/4 cup granulated sugar
1/2 cup packed brown sugar
1/2 cup (1 stick) butter, softened

2 eggs
1 teaspoon vanilla
1 1/2 cups chopped chocolate peanut butter cups (12 to 14 candies)
1 cup dry roasted peanuts

1. Preheat oven to 350°F. Line cookie sheets with parchment paper.

2. Combine flour, baking soda and salt in medium bowl; mix well.

3. Beat peanut butter, granulated sugar, brown sugar and butter in large bowl with electric mixer at medium speed about 3 minutes or until creamy. Beat in eggs and vanilla. Add flour mixture; beat until well blended. Stir in chopped candy and peanuts. Drop dough by rounded tablespoonfuls 2 inches apart onto prepared cookie sheets.

4. Bake 13 minutes or until set. Cool on cookie sheets 1 minute; remove to wire racks to cool completely.

Apple Cranberry Crumble

MAKES 4 SERVINGS

4 large apples (about 1⅓ pounds), peeled and cut into ¼-inch slices

2 cups fresh or frozen cranberries

⅓ cup granulated sugar

6 tablespoons all-purpose flour, divided

1 teaspoon apple pie spice, divided

¼ teaspoon salt, divided

½ cup chopped walnuts

¼ cup old-fashioned oats

2 tablespoons packed brown sugar

¼ cup (½ stick) butter, cut into small pieces

1. Preheat oven to 375°F.

2. Combine apples, cranberries, granulated sugar, 2 tablespoons flour, ½ teaspoon apple pie spice and ⅛ teaspoon salt in large bowl; toss to coat. Spoon into medium (8- to 9-inch) ovenproof skillet.

3. Combine remaining 4 tablespoons flour, ½ teaspoon apple pie spice, ⅛ teaspoon salt, walnuts, oats and brown sugar in medium bowl; mix well. Cut in butter with pastry blender or two knives until mixture resembles coarse crumbs. Sprinkle over fruit mixture in skillet.

4. Bake 50 to 60 minutes or until filling is bubbly and topping is lightly browned.

Classic Chocolate Birthday Cake

MAKES 12 TO 16 SERVINGS

2 cups all-purpose flour

3¼ cups sugar, divided

⅔ cup unsweetened cocoa powder

2 teaspoons baking soda

1½ teaspoons baking powder

¾ teaspoon salt

1¾ cups buttermilk

½ cup vegetable oil

2 eggs

2 teaspoons vanilla, divided

6 ounces unsweetened chocolate, chopped

½ cup (1 stick) butter, cut into small pieces

1 cup whipping cream

1. Preheat oven to 350°F. Line bottoms of two 9-inch cake pans with parchment paper; spray pans and paper with nonstick cooking spray.

2. Combine flour, 1¾ cups sugar, cocoa, baking soda, baking powder and salt in large bowl; mix well. Whisk buttermilk, oil, eggs and 1 teaspoon vanilla in medium bowl until well blended. Stir into flour mixture until well blended. Divide batter between prepared pans.

3. Bake 22 to 24 minutes or until toothpick inserted into centers comes out clean. Cool in pans 10 minutes; remove to wire racks to cool completely.

4. Combine chocolate and butter in medium bowl. Heat remaining 1½ cups sugar and cream in small saucepan over medium-high heat, stirring until sugar is dissolved. When cream begins to bubble, reduce heat and simmer 5 minutes. Pour over chocolate and butter; stir until smooth. Stir in remaining 1 teaspoon vanilla. Refrigerate until frosting is cool and thickened, stirring occasionally.

5. Place one cake layer on serving plate; spread with 1 cup frosting. Top with second cake layer; frost top and side of cake with remaining frosting. Refrigerate at least 1 hour before slicing. Refrigerate leftovers.

188

Metric Conversion Chart

VOLUME MEASUREMENTS (dry)

¹/₈ teaspoon = 0.5 mL
¹/₄ teaspoon = 1 mL
¹/₂ teaspoon = 2 mL
³/₄ teaspoon = 4 mL
1 teaspoon = 5 mL
1 tablespoon = 15 mL
2 tablespoons = 30 mL
¹/₄ cup = 60 mL
¹/₃ cup = 75 mL
¹/₂ cup = 125 mL
²/₃ cup = 150 mL
³/₄ cup = 175 mL
1 cup = 250 mL
2 cups = 1 pint = 500 mL
3 cups = 750 mL
4 cups = 1 quart = 1 L

VOLUME MEASUREMENTS (fluid)

1 fluid ounce (2 tablespoons) = 30 mL
4 fluid ounces (¹/₂ cup) = 125 mL
8 fluid ounces (1 cup) = 250 mL
12 fluid ounces (1¹/₂ cups) = 375 mL
16 fluid ounces (2 cups) = 500 mL

WEIGHTS (mass)

¹/₂ ounce = 15 g
1 ounce = 30 g
3 ounces = 90 g
4 ounces = 120 g
8 ounces = 225 g
10 ounces = 285 g
12 ounces = 360 g
16 ounces = 1 pound = 450 g

DIMENSIONS

¹/₁₆ inch = 2 mm
¹/₈ inch = 3 mm
¹/₄ inch = 6 mm
¹/₂ inch = 1.5 cm
³/₄ inch = 2 cm
1 inch = 2.5 cm

OVEN TEMPERATURES

250°F = 120°C
275°F = 140°C
300°F = 150°C
325°F = 160°C
350°F = 180°C
375°F = 190°C
400°F = 200°C
425°F = 220°C
450°F = 230°C

BAKING PAN SIZES

Utensil	Size in Inches/Quarts	Metric Volume	Size in Centimeters
Baking or Cake Pan (square or rectangular)	8×8×2	2 L	20×20×5
	9×9×2	2.5 L	23×23×5
	12×8×2	3 L	30×20×5
	13×9×2	3.5 L	33×23×5
Loaf Pan	8×4×3	1.5 L	20×10×7
	9×5×3	2 L	23×13×7
Round Layer Cake Pan	8×1½	1.2 L	20×4
	9×1½	1.5 L	23×4
Pie Plate	8×1¼	750 mL	20×3
	9×1¼	1 L	23×3
Baking Dish or Casserole	1 quart	1 L	—
	1½ quart	1.5 L	—
	2 quart	2 L	—